Now and Then

EMILY KIMBROUGH

Now and Then

Drawings by Mircea Vasiliu

HARPER & ROW, PUBLISHERS

New York, Evanston, San Francisco, London

The selection from "Dear Abby" on the last page is reprinted through the courtesy of the Chicago Tribune–New York News Syndicate, Inc.

NOW AND THEN. Copyright © 1972 by Emily Kimbrough. All rights reserved. Printed in the United States of America. No part of this book may be used or reproduced in any manner whatsoever without written permission except in the case of brief quotations embodied in critical articles and reviews. For information address Harper & Row, Publishers, Inc., 10 East 53rd Street, New York, N.Y. 10022. Published simultaneously in Canada by Fitzhenry & Whiteside Limited, Toronto.

FIRST EDITION

STANDARD BOOK NUMBER: 06-012366-4

LIBRARY OF CONGRESS CATALOG CARD NUMBER: 72-79678

Designed by Pat Dunbar

To Alis (A.) and Margaret (B.)
with love

Contents

Now and Then

I

Double Image

Agatha Christie's astute spinster Jane Marple solved mysteries Scotland Yard's best could not penetrate, by linking each one to an incident in the village in which she lived. The village incident was too unimportant for even the notice of the local constabulary but Miss Marple, like a good cook tasting a new dish, could identify the basic ingredients and prove them to be identical in a simple village incident and a very fancy crime.

Of course Miss Marple's pattern of association had nothing to do with having twins. I apologize for even mentioning such an indelicate impossibility, but I have wondered if somewhere between the spinster, for whom the life of her community supplants a family, and a mother of twins there is a common denominator.

A mother of twins sees and thinks in double images; this stems from the necessity of double dealing. She sees two cribs, proffers two bottles, holds two babies. (In order to keep a hand free and useful, I learned to carry twins single file down and over one arm.) I think I am speaking for all such mothers when I make these assertions of division and multiplication though I have not done any research. In a library I would not know under what category to look for such data and I cannot compare my own findings with other mothers of twins, because I do not know any. My friends have had and brought up their children one at a time. Paradoxically, I have met, I think without exaggeration, hundreds of mothers in my category, but always under particular circumstances that make our meeting a brief encounter.

Twice a year I hit the creamed-chicken trail of speaking engagements. My topics vary, but invariably, for all my determination against it, I insert some mention of, or anecdote about, my twin daughters. If I were to ask urgently if there was a doctor in the audience, I could scarcely have a more immediate response. The only difference is the time lag. A doctor would stand up at once; a mother of twins—and sometimes there is a handful of them—is at my side as I leave the platform. I recognize them at once. We shake hands conventionally, but strong as a fraternity grip, there is an unexpressed wink of the eye and nudge in the ribs. We are "sports." If having twins is not sufficient mutation for us to qualify biologically as such, we are "different," and certainly qualify for synonyms of the other kind of sport—"showy," even "raffish."

We have time only for a quick exchange. The opening is usually:

"How do you feel when other women, outsiders, say, 'I envy your having twins. It must be so much easier.'?"

We smile understandingly at each other, and she moves on. I know her answer to this silly question would agree with mine, less violently expressed probably, and perhaps not accompanied by an impulse to do bodily harm to the nincompoop who has said such a silly thing.

There's nothing "easier" about having twins, from the burgeoning period straight on.

If my sisters in the sorority of mothers of twins look about my age, I know our bond is extra strong. Our pairs were born in the era of rigid schedules. If one baby woke fifteen minutes before bottle time the awakening was clarioned. This promptly roused the other to matching decibels and both screamed until the clock permitted them to be picked up, changed and fed—simultaneously. One compensation this era allowed was a nurse. Mine, young, warm, loving with babies, was German, trained in a children's hospital at Stuttgart. What a doctor said must be followed with scrupulous precision, and no lag. Therefore she "did" one baby, I the other; when the first was bottled she was handed to me to dress and put in her crib. While I dressed the second, Alma heated the bottles. With not a second between, each open mouth held a nipple, or a sodden glob of spinach. Services had not caught up with system. We had no Didee Wash— let alone Throwaways; between fifty and sixty pennants waved on the line every day. The special foods were prepared by Alma, with strainers and mashers for vegetables and pressers for extracting meat juices.

Given more time than our brief encounters allowed, we contemporaries would have asked one another why we allowed ourselves to be so persecuted by a system. We were fools, of course, but we were young and scared. We put ourselves and our frail little bundles under the care of a pediatrician. We had neither knowledge nor courage to gainsay him. Babies are tough. They grow up. How parents survive is the miracle, but they had grown up by the time we caught on to that. For three nights or more in a row, wrapped in a comforter I have sat in a room where a croup kettle steamed and listened to breathing that sounded like rusty

4

gate latches opening. Alma and I would take turns of perhaps two hours, allowing each other that much sleep. There always came a morning, thank God, when one could rouse the other with:

"The babies are fine. They've had a big breakfast. They want to get out of their cribs, and play."

We would have been happy to stay in our beds for a week, and sleep.

Every mother has known those nights and days, but every mother has not known double double toil and trouble.

That stage passed, we came to the phase—and it was not a passing one—of separate but equal. How it simplifies shopping and choosing to buy duplicate Christmas or birthday presents for twins. How twins hate it. Unless they count together, "One, two, three, *open*," one has no surprise from a package. My twins demanded birthday guests separately chosen—sometimes by drawing from names on slips of paper in my hand—two tables, the favors and decorations on each different from the other, and birthday cakes of individual shape and color, but certainly exactly the same size.

Did those women who tell us twins are "easier" consider the economic "ease," we special mothers ask ourselves. A twin does not fall heir to the outgrown clothes or possessions of the other. Two bicycles are purchased simultaneously, sleds, writing desks. The list is heavy; so are the expenditures.

We would not change our double standard for any gold, but it is *not* "easy" to maintain. To keep an even balance makes the tightrope walker in a circus, by comparison, a bumbling amateur.

Those are the things I know I share with the women who identify themselves as gemini bearers, clasp my hand with understanding pressure and move on. These are the things I wish there were time to ask:

5

Do they pair off instantly in their minds one incident with another, different but similar? I know a universal trait is expressed by "That reminds me," but do the reminder and the incident occur simultaneously? They do for me. I think the reason is my conditioning that began at the double birth and will last my life. I never telephone one of my daughters, I always call each of them. Is this perhaps why, weekly, I talk to my stepmother in California and my brother in Chicago, one immediately following the other? It occurs to me, as I review these idiosyncrasies, I invariably read two books simultaneously, though not literally one in each hand. Reading, hearing or telling, I like balancing one story with another.

When my twins were three years old, I took them one day in December to a Christmas play at a nearby school. It was the first play they had seen, and they sat wide-eyed, remarkably still. The following afternoon I was called urgently to the playroom. One child sat on a low stool beside a doll's bed. Over her shoulders was draped a blue dressing gown of mine that lay in folds, like a robe, around her feet. On her head she wore a towel that hung down on either side of her face. She held upright in hand a stick from a drum, evidently a candle. Leaning toward the bed tenderly, she sat motionless. Lying on the bed, side by side, were two stuffed animals.

The other participant seemed to be the impresario and interpreter. Pointing to the tableau, she announced with measured solemnity, as she had heard the day before:

"Here is Mary with the little Lord Jesus—and his twin," she added.

For these two spectators there had been two babes in the manger at the play. They had actually not seen only one.

They have taught me to see and hear by twos.

7

II

Cases of Detection

One Sunday recently my two daughters and I watched on television the World Ice Skating Championship. My twin daughters are deeply involved in the sport. One is a teacher; the other, who did not turn professional, is now a national judge. All the years they were growing up I was an ice skating mother. A skating mother I venture to say is unique in the world of sport: at least I have never heard of tennis or golf mothers. Our not so happy breed wears stadium boots, heavy coats with sweaters underneath, a scarf over the head and warm gloves whether it is July at Lake Placid or mid-winter at the home club. Hunched with cold we sit on a bench or a camp stool as close as permitted to that section of the vast field of ice before us known as a "patch." It has been reserved for the offspring who is having a lesson or is engaged in what is called a practice session. At these sessions, because we have followed the lessons we call out expert advice: "Keep your right shoulder down, bring that left hip in a little."

With few exceptions not one of us, if we were to put on

skates with double runners, could stand, let alone take a step, unsupported on the ice.

Dick Button was a commentator for this event. I am reasonably sure he was christened Richard, but I have never known him to be introduced as other than Dick. When we first knew him he was ten years old and called Dickie. Among his qualifications as a commentator are the statistics that he was twice a gold medalist in the Olympic Championships, won the National Championship in ice skating six years in a row, and chalked up the same consecutive record in the World Championships. As he finished explaining to the viewers points of technique in the event at the moment completed, B, one of my daughters, said:

"Do you remember when I got the mumps?"

She was looking at me, and I nodded. We shared a secret. She turned back to the screen.

Like Dick Button, B has a christening name that is never used. It happens to be Margaret. She is called B because she is a twin and her twin sister is called A. I vouchsafe an explanation of this even without being asked because I wince at a possible implication of "cuteness" or "whimsy." The reason for the abbreviated and particular nomenclature was both practical and unself-conscious.

The announcement that I had been delivered of twins came as a great surprise to their father and me. We had not prepared ourselves with names for two. As I daresay is still the custom, a bracelet was put on each infant. The bracelet was composed of beads each imprinted with a letter to spell, as identification, the last name. Since in this double situation the last name was insufficient, the letter A was added to one and B to the other. With a special precision of data, it was pointed out to me afterward, B also stood for the earlier arrival by ten minutes and therefore could be interpreted as before A; B has always insisted on a recognition of this seniority. Today these souvenirs would be discarded and dismembered, I suppose, within forty-eight hours, when the mother left the hospital. In those far-off and, to me, happy times, a mother stayed in the hospital for at least two weeks, was cosseted by her own trained nurse, and took the nurse home. Mine had the most beautiful fit of name to personality I have ever known. She was Mrs. Devine. In her many years of nursing experience these were her first twins. Afraid she might bring the same one in twice for a feeding, though I knew them apart from the moment they were presented to me, she paid exaggerated attention to the charts. Each time, arriving at my room from the hospital nursery, she would look at the bracelet before saying:

"I've brought you A" or "I've brought you B."

Mrs. Devine stayed with us for eight weeks. In the meantime there had been a christening in which A had become Alis and B, Margaret, but when Mrs. Devine left, the bracelet names were indelibly stamped on our tongues. They are B and A to this day. To each other's children they are Aunt B and Aunt A. Though each has black hair and blue eyes, their children have never confused their identities any more than their mother ever confused them.

For B to ask if I remembered when she had the mumps was as rhetorical a question as if she had asked me to remember when she and her twin were born.

It was a night in April when B's mumps began. The twins were twelve years old and we were on a train traveling from Muncie, Indiana, home to Philadelphia. The trip had been my proposal, a sentimental journey. I had been on a speaking tour and my final engagement was in Muncie, the town in which I was born. The sight of this on my itinerary prompted what seemed to me at the time a lovely idea and before I left home I made all the preparations to have it carried out. The twins were to be excused from school on Friday, and put on a train Thursday night. I would meet them in Muncie the day of my speaking engagement; they would be excused from that on their own request. We would then have the weekend, when they would come to know my roots and theirs. They had visited Muncie when they were a year and half old and again at five but had not been back since then. The memory of a five-year-old is quixotic. Theirs ranged from strawberry shortcake made of pie crust, which is the way we do it in Indiana, to a candy Mr. Roller made that merited national fame. It was called a Dark Secret. So was the twins' memory between it and the strawberry shortcake.

My plan unrolled as smoothly as a wedding carpet down the aisle of a church. Why I did not accept this tranquillity with foreboding I do not know. I should have recognized the stillness before a storm and braced myself, because in my pattern of living I have only to originate a scheme, work out in advance every detail toward its accomplishment, to have it blow up at the moment of execution. My well-laid plans do not gang a-gley; they explode. This one had gone from idea to accomplishment without a hitch and I had enjoyed it without misgiving; I must have been stultified by the rich food we ate.

My girls had a wonderful time. They fell in with their contemporaries and their contemporaries took to them, a remarkable occurrence, I think, because usually the children of friends hate one another on sight or even before. The only complaint voiced by mine, not so much a complaint as a request for praise of their docile acceptance, was that they had never been kissed so much and by so many people in all their lives; and certainly, born and brought up in Philadelphia, had not been told once, let alone numerous times a day, how much they resembled in one way or another their Muncie grandparents and great-grandparents.

A sizable crowd came to the station to see us off; not so large as waves to departing royalty, but gratifying and truly heartwarming. There was of course another round of kissing before we boarded the train.

Sometime in the night B woke her sister and me; we were sharing a compartment. The braces on her teeth had slipped, she told us, and were giving her terrible pain. I filled the hot water bottle I always carry with me, applied it to her face, and she went back to sleep but not for long. Throughout the rest of the night she was up with me or across with A. I rubbed her back and refilled the hot water bottle. When we came into Paoli station at about half past seven the next morning A and I were groggy from want of sleep and B was still in pain. I told them I would telephone the school as soon as we got home to have them excused for another day. Instead of leaving the house again once we had reached it, we would do better to stop off at Dr. Sturgis's office since this was the day they were due for a shot, what kind of shot I do not now remember. I do remember vividly, however, that as part of my well-organized plan I had, before leaving on the tour, engaged Roy Johnson, our local Bryn Mawr taxi man, to meet this train; he had first met me at trains when I was in boarding school in Bryn Mawr. He wanted to know if the children had enjoyed their trip to their mother's hometown. A was volubly enthusiastic but B sat miserably quiet. I explained to Roy her braces had slipped and that her mouth hurt badly. Roy was sympathetic and helpful. Why didn't he drive us home after a stop at Dr. Sturgis's, drop off A and then take B and me straight into town to the "brace man"? We probably would only be a few minutes there. Just a little screwing and unscrewing—B groaned—and then he'd bring us right back home, where we could settle for a good rest. I endorsed the suggestion.

The doctor's nurse gave the required shot, but as we were leaving Dr. Sturgis came from his inner office to ask how the twins had liked Muncie, surmising, he said, they must have met everybody in the town.

"Not the whole town maybe," A told him, "but everybody we did meet kissed us." She shuddered extravagantly. "It was fun though," she added.

Again I explained B's silence, adding we were on our way now to get the brace put back in place, Roy Johnson was waiting. Dr. Sturgis said he was glad it was nothing more than a slipped brace and stopped abruptly.

"Hold on a moment," he said. He had been shaking hands with B and patting her commiseratingly on the shoulder. A and I were already out the door and he called us back. He led B to a light on the nurse's desk, tilted the lamp up toward her face, turned her head from side to side, felt gently under the line of her jaw; she winced. He looked across her at me.

"Don't bother to go in town," he said. "Just get this child home and to bed; I'll be over later. She's got a double case of mumps, both sides."

If I said anything I have forgotten it, but I can almost still feel the shock and the numbness that followed his news. Probably it was stupid of me not to have thought of such a possibility, but B had said her braces slipped, that was where it hurt, and I had accepted it; furthermore, neither of the children had reported any case of mumps at school. I do not suppose I thought of these things at the moment. I stood like a pillar of salt in the corridor outside Dr. Sturgis's office. Though it seems unlikely, considering the nature of the child, I do not remember that even A said anything. B was crying a little and I think I had my arm around her. I have every reason to remember, however, what Dr. Sturgis called after us as we reached the door. He was a jovial man.

"Nice to know you kissed nearly everybody in Muncie."

A's response has stayed in my memory because it seems now as adequate an appraisal of the situation as could have been offered.

"Golly gee." I had nothing to add.

Roy's comment on the change of plan and the reason for it was a long whistle on a descending scale. That too seemed a good summing up of everything involved.

B's was a light case. In a few days she was out of bed, and a week after the swelling was gone, by Board of Health rules, she was back at school. By the same rules, from the fourteenth to the twenty-first day, A had to leave school and with me be put in quarantine. I wrote all the people in Muncie who had been so kind to us, miserably giving them the news of how we were repaying their hospitality. By the time we were out of quarantine I had had a good many answers admitting that the memory of our stay was vivid, widespread and never to be forgotten.

On the twenty-first day, the period of incubation ended; A and I were released. The date of A's and my return to the outside world coincided with Parents' Day at the school. The children and I went together that morning. I visited each of their classes, talked to every teacher. It was a happy day. After school we went to Best's store in Ardmore, the suburb next to Haverford, where we lived. Summer was adjacent too, and the twins needed clothes for it. Evidently a great many children on the Main Line had the same need; the shop was crowded with them and their mothers, most of whom we knew and chatted with.

That night I went to the theater in Philadelphia. Friends were making this a party of theater and supper afterward to celebrate my return from the cloister of sickroom and quarantine. We were eight so we drove in two cars, one of them mine. I do not remember the play but I know I was enjoying it thoroughly when shortly after the intermission, which had given me an opportunity to see and talk with other friends there that night, I suddenly experienced how it must feel to be "socked in the jaw." Astonished at so unlikely an occurrence in a theater, and certainly with no visible assailant, I instinctively put my hand to the spot that had been assaulted. An unmistakable swelling burgeoned under my hand. I knew what, not who, had attacked me, and I echoed to myself A's summary "Golly gee."

After my whispered announcement to my neighbor and a vehement injunction not to come with me, I managed to get away unaccompanied. I think the others were not so much cowed by my vehemence as by the indignant hissing from other audience members in front of and behind us. On the way home, somewhere in Fairmont Park, I was clouted again on the other side and I remember vividly the eerie experience of feeling another swelling grow underneath my hand. Except for my aching jaws I had no feeling of illness, fever, chills, headache. I would have welcomed any of these distractions from the appalling realization of the second round of letters I must write, this time to the school, to the friends with whom I had talked during the afternoon at Best's, others in the lobby of the theater. And what to say to the friends who had given the theater party? I was still making and discarding phrases while I put the car in the garage, walked back down the driveway and let myself into the house. A provided an immediate distraction as I closed the front door behind me. Her room was on the third floor; she was leaning over the stairs. She called down.

"Mommy, is that you? I'm sick."

"We both are," I told her. "I'm coming right up."

Once, in Paris, I fell down a flight of stone steps and suffered a concussion that wiped out all memory of what had preceded and what followed as well as the occurrence itself. No such benevolent oblivion accompanied my encounter with mumps. Mine was the most severe case he had ever encountered, Dr. Sturgis told me, adding that he had seen plenty. In the First World War at the hospital in which he served there had been under his care an epidemic of the disease, with two wards filled to more than capacity. Not one of them matched mine in circumference.

Apart from the acute pain it brings, mumps is a humiliating, ignominious affliction. Instead of lying wan and frail, whispering brave words of encouragement to my dear ones, whose faces were pinched with anxiety as they bent over me, I sat upright in bed day and night because it hurt more to lean against a pillow. I wore a scarf folded under my chin, the ends tied on top of my head, because, I reasoned, since old engravings invariably identified similar sufferers by a sling of this kind, there must have been a reason for it. There was, and I found it a good one. The sling bolstered up and relieved the pressure of the drooping jowls. Dear ones came to the bedside, but their faces were not pinched with anxiety; they were contorted by an effort to conceal and stifle coarse laughter.

A's case was as light as B's had been. The epidemic we provoked, though not so widespread as the one B had kindled in Muncie, penetrated more deeply into the events it influenced. The graduation at the school had to be postponed because the school was in quarantine. A sizable number of parents of seniors were taking their girls abroad as a graduation present; they were unable to change the sailing dates; the trips had to be canceled. The harvest of our sowing was more widespread geographically, too, than the one in Muncie because the twins' was both a boarding and a day school for girls. Relatives of the seniors were coming to the graduation from all parts of the country and could not accommodate to the change of calendar. Even as I write it so long after the memory of what we wreaked, I wince with shame and move on rapidly to Dr. Sturgis.

From the day he had first come to see B, not more than an hour after we had left his office, he had begun to question her about places she had been and friends she had seen. In the intervening hours he had checked with the Health Department and found no cases of mumps reported in the township nor over a considerable area beyond. She must have caught it somewhere beyond this vicinity, yet not in Muncie because the visit there was too short and the time of her coming down with the disease of too immediate sequence.

From the first questioning B insisted she had gone nowhere outside Philadelphia except to Muncie and I could verify it. Dr. Sturgis accepted this with reservations. He was a persistent and perceptive man and he had known the children from birth. The children loved him; he was my mainstay and counselor. After the second or third visit to B, when he had asked the same questions as he went over her, he had indicated he wanted to speak to me. I went downstairs with him and we talked, while B could hear us, of details of treatment and diet. At the front door, when we were out of earshot, he looked at me quizzically.

"I think B is holding out on us," he said. "There's something she doesn't want to tell."

He was more perceptive than I, or perhaps, in justification, I was too preoccupied with her misery and how to make her more comfortable.

When she had bounced back to health, as children do almost overnight, I thought I detected in her an evasiveness and a discomfort that was not physical, though I was not sure my suspicions were genuine and not implanted by Dr. Sturgis. In the interim between B's recovery and my succumbing, his visits and the questioning stopped, but both were resumed when A and I inaugurated the second round. This time there was no doubt about B's evasiveness and her unhappiness. The severity of my attack required the services of a nurse at Dr. Sturgis's order. B's insistence on helping did not make it easier for Miss Smith to render these services. B trailed her, asking at intervals of minutes if she thought I was feeling any better. She begged to be allowed to help in whatever Miss Smith was doing and to stay in the room, except when she heard Dr. Sturgis's step and voice announcing his approach. Then she would shoot out, pounding up the stairs to her room on the third floor. Miss Smith would mercifully be unattended until B was sure the doctor had gone. She gave A solicitous attention too but since A's case, like her own, was short-lived, and A out of bed in a few days, I was the victim of her devotion.

The first day A was well enough to come down to see me, she stared for an instant and then shouted joyous laughter at the sight. B kicked her in the shins. B's devotion was touch-

ing and wearisome, but I was too sick to be stern in my request that she go away. As I emerged from my self-preoccupation enough to care about anyone else, I realized B did not look well; that A, more recently recovered from mumps, looked better than she. At Dr. Sturgis's next visit I asked if he would take a look at her.

"Her behavior is touching but unnatural," I told him, "and I don't like the way she looks."

Dr. Sturgis with satisfaction nodded agreement.

"She's got something on her mind she's hiding, and it's something to do with the mumps. Let's get her down here and talk to her if you feel up to it."

Miss Smith was sent to fetch her and returned with the message B was sorry, she was very busy and could not come. At that moment I knew I was better and was going to get well soon. I lifted my voice to the third floor in a tone that brought B down. Miss Smith was sent on an errand. A was outside.

Dr. Sturgis placed a chair between the one he was occupying and my bed, B was invited to sit between her two inquisitors. She hesitated a moment but catching my eye, sat down. Her eyes were big; she looked at me pleadingly and then defiantly, her body stiffening. My feelings were as divided as her expression. I wanted to take her on the bed beside me and put my arms around her; at the same time I felt respect for her fortitude. Evidently Dr. Sturgis shared something of this; his voice was gentle. He said, I remember, something like this:

"B, we know there's something you haven't told your mother and me and we know it's bothering you. We're pretty sure it has something to do with your getting the mumps. If it has, I really need to know about it, because,

21

you see, if you had told us in the beginning that you'd been exposed—and something tells me you knew you had been"—he waited; B made no answer—"then I would have kept you at home for the time when you might have come down with it." He smiled at her. She was looking directly at him. "Maybe you knew that would happen and didn't want to miss the Muncie trip?"

B shook her head with positive denial.

"But you see," Dr. Sturgis continued, "you gave it to a lot of other people and I'm sure you haven't been happy about that. It's really why Mother and I are asking you to tell us about it. I would like to report it to the Board of Health to make the record complete, but I truly care much more about your being happy again. Then you'll be really all well and we'll forget the whole thing."

B turned to look at me and I nodded.

The silence was broken by a wail that rivaled commendably the siren on an ambulance. I am sure Dr. Sturgis jumped. I, leaning tenderly over my child, very nearly fell out of bed into her lap. While I was recovering my balance she buried her head in the comforter, sobbing and talking at the same time. It was not easy to distinguish the words but I remember them.

"Any other girl could kiss a boy for the first time and not have it spread all over the country. Lots of girls kiss boys and they don't have to tell it to the Board of Health, and he lives in New Jersey anyway. But I didn't want you to be sick, Mommy, or A or all those other people and have it be all my fault. Oh, I feel awful."

Dr. Sturgis stood up, patting B on the back. He looked across at me with a facial contortion I had seen on sickroom visitors trying not to laugh at my appearance.

"Listen, B," he said when he could speak. "Don't feel awful; you're going to feel fine now and it's all over." He walked away, turning back at the door. "And one more thing. This will not be reported to our Board of Health."

When he had gone B raised her head. She was crying less violently. I wiped her face and gave her another Kleenex to blow her nose. The sobs she was checking made her speech ragged but she wanted to talk.

"You took us to the movies in Ardmore and then you came for us. We got out before you came and we were in that driveway along the side entrance and it was dark. I didn't know he was going to but he kissed me"—she paused —"and I kissed back."

"Good for you," I told her.

Her eyes widened and she grinned a little, pleased, surprised. "Well, then." She stopped to swallow, take a breath; the speech was smoother now. "He went home Sunday night. He was only here for the weekend for his skating lessons and that very Sunday night when he got home he came down with the mumps. So he wrote to me and said he thought he ought to tell me because he thought I'd better tell you." Another siren wail interrupted her but she spoke through it. "That's just what I didn't want to do because I'd have had to tell you about the kissing and don't you know when you kiss somebody it's very private? You don't want to go telling it around. That's why on the train I really thought my brace had slipped. Mumps didn't come into my mind at all. It was such ages since, you know, the kissing—I just forgot about the mumps part. I didn't know you had to wait so long. I never prayed so hard in my life as I did in the beginning and sure enough I didn't get it. So then I didn't think about it any more. I guess the reason the praying was no good was it wasn't really right. Then when I did get it and after that when you got so sick I knew it was punishment for not telling."

It was all so logical to a twelve-year-old; certainly twenty-one days one after another makes ages. And if a dreaded event does not happen immediately it is not going to happen at all. Punishment and the form it took was thoroughly logical too.

"Well, if all this was punishment," I told her, "you've had it. Go on upstairs; wash your face."

B jumped up, leaned over, flung her arms around my neck, kissed me.

"Does A have to know?" she asked. "It's the first thing I ever kept from her but my whole life would be ruined if people knew."

"A won't know," I promised, "nor anybody else. Dr. Sturgis won't tell. By the way," I added as she skipped toward the door, "do you mind telling me who the boy was? You don't have to."

"Why, Dickie Button, of course," she said.

The intermission and the commercials in the televised Skating Championship had come and gone. My girls were absorbed again in the program, Dick Button analyzing each coming figure. For me the image on the screen faded to another memory of another doctor detective, to Dr. Cowing and me on the stairs in Grandfather's house on the day he asked if I remembered when my brother had diphtheria. In the years between it had gone into one of the dark closets of my memory, like a single overshoe that gets pushed into a corner by rubbers that match until one day another single appears. The old one is rummaged for, brought out, and they make a pair. Sunday afternoon when I relived the humiliating episode of the mumps, Dr. Cowing's story came out of the dark corner and matched Dr. Sturgis's in persistence and detection.

Dr. Cowing had been our family doctor in Muncie. Physically there was no resemblance between him and Dr. Sturgis. Dr. Sturgis was not tall; he moved and spoke quickly. His voice was decisive and high. His ancestry was Swedish, he had told me; his blue eyes corroborated this, though his hair was light brown. Dr. Cowing was tall; perhaps he only seemed so because I was small when I knew him. His eyes were dark, I think. I know he wore gold spectacles. He moved slowly and spoke slowly too, in a deep voice. Later I could have identified his as the typical Indiana measured speech.

I was eleven when we moved to Chicago, but whenever I came back to Muncie for a visit at my grandparents' I always saw him. He used to drop by to see Grandfather, not professionally, Grandmother said; it was because they both served on several committees and Grandfather was head of the hospital board, so they had lots to talk about whenever the doctor had a few minutes to spare. She would say:

"Charles is in the den, doctor. Go right on back."

To reach the den after he had stopped in the vestibule to take off his hat and coat, putting them on a bench there, he had to walk the length of a wide hall. It was a room in itself with a fireplace, a couch facing it, and comfortable chairs. On the left was the library and on the right the parlor, where the piano was, and alongside it a pianola, that could be attached to the keyboard. The dining room was behind the library, the den across from it with the stairs between. Each opened off the hall. The den was the only room in the house in which Grandmother permitted the men to smoke;

Grandfather spent most of his time there. Halfway up the stairs there was a landing with a balcony that jutted out over the downstairs hall. This was a favorite place of mine for reading. There was enough light for it from the windows at the top of the stairs, and incongruously, on the balcony itself there was a little upholstered settee with cushions across its back. I do not suppose anyone ever sat there, I cannot imagine for what purpose one would have, but I liked it. With some contortion of my legs I could lie on it. Perhaps I imagined I was in a tower, I do not remember; but I do remember the day I called down to Dr. Cowing as he was on his way to the den. I think I was pleased that I startled him but what indented the day and the place in my memory was what he told me. He asked what I was reading and I said Sherlock Holmes.

"Once I was a detective," he said, "at your house when you lived here in Muncie. When I've seen your grandfather, if I have time I'll tell you about it."

When he left the den some time later he did have time. I came down from the balcony, sat on one of the lower steps of the stairs, and he sat down beside me to tell the story. That is probably what has left me with the conviction he was tall because I remember sitting on one step with my feet on the one below, while his legs stretched from beside me down to and across the floor. He began the story by asking if I remembered when my brother had had diphtheria.

Certainly I remembered. Brother was three and I was "going on" nine and I reminded Dr. Cowing I had had diphtheria too. Admitting this, he gave it small importance.

"A very light case," he said.

It had not been a light occurrence in my life; had I known the word at the time, I would have called it a disaster. There was to be an entertainment at our church at night. To be taken to anything in the evening would have been a heady experience but there was more. I was not only to be taken, I was to be in it, conspicuously. I was to wear a dress of my great-grandmother Curry's, who was eighty-eight years old, "lively as a cricket," people said, and not much taller than I was. I was to have my hair put up on top of my head and on that wear one of Grandmother Curry's little flat lace caps. I was to sit beside a make-believe fire and sing a solo, with Mother at the piano offstage. To my knowledge I have not rendered the song since then, but even today I know all the words. The selection was "Just a Song at Twilight" and it began "Just a song at twilight, when the lights are low, And the flickering shadows softly come and go." I did not sing the song, I was not even taken to the entertainment, because I caught diphtheria from my brother. I know to this day, as vividly as I know the words of that song, the fury and despair I could not shout to the housetop and everyone under it because my throat hurt.

"Yes, you caught diphtheria from little Charles but where had he caught it? That's when I turned into a detective. You see, diphtheria was one of the most terrible diseases that could happen in a family. When there was an epidemic many people died. One time in a family of nine children I could only save one." He did not speak for a moment and I tried to imagine such a dreadful time.

"In many churches ministers prayed diphtheria would not strike. The time I'm going to tell you about, it did strike, but only once, and that was your little brother—and you, of course," he added. Only my interest in the story kept me from reminding him sharply of the importance of my case.

"To this day I don't know what made me sure as soon as I

saw him that Charles had diphtheria. They were such early symptoms I could easily have mistaken it for tonsillitis, especially since there had been no case of diphtheria reported."

He had seemed to be talking to himself. He turned back to me. "Anyway I took a culture but I didn't wait for it to develop. I telephoned Chicago for antitoxin. We didn't have any in Muncie because as I told you there was no epidemic, not even one other case reported. They rushed the antitoxin from Chicago on a train in the special care of the conductor. Your father was waiting at the station and brought it straight to me. I heard later mine was the largest amount that had ever been given to a child up to that time but I took the risk, I had to, and we pulled him through.

"It was when he was getting better I turned into a detective."

Dr. Cowing was a good storyteller. He did not make gestures, he did not even raise his voice, but there was something in the slow, thoughtful speech that made my spine shiver. I remember that and almost exactly the very words he used.

"Where could a child of three have been exposed to diphtheria? Over and over I asked myself this question and could not answer it. I asked many people and they could not answer it."

Long after Brother needed his care the doctor had come to the house, he said, to talk to my parents and Zoe, Brother's and my nurse. Mrs. Lothan had gone when Brother was over the worst of the illness. The fact that she had been there at all might have given me realization Brother was very ill had I not been preoccupied with my own resentment. She was Dr. Cowing's standby. Together they had brought into the world a sizable proportion of Muncie's population and she was the one always sent for in any emergency. She had been of no help, however, in tracing where Brother might have been before she was called in. The one who would know that best was Zoe.

Zoe was colored, "like the tassels on ears of corn," I had said. I loved her and I know she loved me, but Brother was her baby and she was fiercely protective of him. She was the one Dr. Cowing talked to longest and, he said, once she realized there was no faintest blame attached to her, but only an urgent need of her help so that other children would not get so ill as her little Charles had been, she went earnestly, fervently, over every detail of his days. Where they went to walk, whom they saw—very few children because he was not yet of kindergarten age. Dr. Cowing would visit every place she mentioned, asking questions there. If it was a store, had any clerks been absent through illness? Had there been illness in their family that had anything to do with a sore throat? He thought, he said, there might have been a case even lighter than mine so it had been diagnosed as tonsillitis when in reality it could have been diphtheria. He could find no such possibility. He asked other doctors to help him. There were not many in the town, but he had their cooperation although it meant a great deal of extra work, and he had a feeling, he said, they thought he was being something of a crank. After all, there had been no other cases reported. Brother's and mine had been isolated so it was all over. I can hear now the tone of his voice when he added:

"They had never seen a diphtheria epidemic. *I* had."

However, the other doctors took on with him the extra load—and every family doctor's was a heavy load—of examining all the schoolchildren and making inquiries about their families.

In the weeks that followed, while Dr. Cowing was digging for clues Brother was getting well. The afternoon of the denouement, the last page of the detective story, Zoe had just brought him in from outdoor play when Dr. Cowing stopped by. She was taking off his outdoor things and as she released him Dr. Cowing held out his arms, Brother dodged them, laughing, and ran toward the back of the house.

"Stop him," Zoe called. Dropping the coat and leggings to the floor, she started after him but Dr. Cowing, reaching out an arm, had already encircled him and questioningly handed him to Zoe.

Over Brother's roars of protest and flailing fists she raised her voice. "He knows his momma don't allow him in the kitchen this time of day."

The temper outburst was soothed by permission to ride his tricycle in the house so long as he did not go to the kitchen. While he circled precariously around and between them—Dr. Cowing remembered he kept having to pull his long legs up out of the way—Zoe told the reason for the rule about the kitchen.

"Every afternoon Frieda, she's the cook, always has coffee and some kind of sweet cake. She's German. She came to us just before the baby took sick. She started a game with him when she first came. She's crazy about children. The baby remembered the game and the minute he was up he wants to play it some more. But his momma don't want him to."

Dr. Cowing, smiling, asked what the game was.

"I thought probably some kind of hide and seek," he explained to me.

"Why, the baby sits up at the table with her and she takes a spoonful of coffee and then she pretends to give him some from her spoon. She don't actually give him coffee, she just lets him lick the spoon, but she does give him some of her cake and his momma don't want him eating between meals. She don't believe in it and especially since we've had such a hard time getting him to eat after him being so sick."

"At that instant—" I remember how he stopped when he said that and I held my breath.

"At that instant," he repeated, "something scratched my mind. It was no more than that but I said, 'Tell me again, Zoe—about the coffee.'"

"Oh, she don't give him real coffee, she knows he shouldn't drink that. It's just pretend. She lets him lick her spoon."

There it was, what Dr. Cowing all the weeks had been looking for. He knew it before he reached the kitchen. He knew when he saw Frieda what he was going to have to do and he felt sick.

Frieda was young, German, pretty, with bright pink cheeks, soft yellow hair that curled around her face, china blue eyes. She was just twenty, and she was a diphtheria carrier. A culture taken from her throat proved it unquestionably. She had to be institutionalized almost as if she were a leper. She could never work as a cook in a family again; she could never even go to any public eating place. She would be under surveillance. Dr. Cowing had solved the mystery.

Dr. Sturgis had traced the source of B's mumps and B said it had ruined her life. She has forgotten she said that. Dr. Cowing discovered the source of Brother's diphtheria and it ruined Frieda's life.

I do not know who won the Ice Skating Championship.

31

III

Hymn Singing

The day my children's hymn singing and an automobile trip with my grandfather jostled my memory simultaneously, I was on a platform filling a speaking engagement; and I was not talking about my family nor about hymns. I was making a plea to throw out our old methods of teaching foreign languages in this country and teach by ear. The child, by this method, I was saying, would give back exactly what he heard, therefore his accent would be as right as that of the person to whom he was listening. That was the instant when I remembered my children's hymn singing and simultaneously the trip with Grandfather when he and I had sung hymns together. For the strength of my argument of exact reproduction of speech heard, I did not share my memories with my audience. I put them resolutely out of my mind and completed the talk I had been engaged to deliver. Later, alone in my hotel room, I savored them both and now they are linked irrevocably.

At the time I was remembering, my twins were not quite five years old. To many people they looked alike, black curly hair, blue eyes, chubby. Most of the time they were compatible though temperamentally quite unlike; B was the more gregarious. In one activity, however—I cannot diminish its importance by calling it a game—even B eschewed friends. To be accurate, the activity combined two forms of expression; neither was engaged in separately. At nursery school they played singing games and sang marching songs, but the home entertainment was singing and marching. From the volume of sound each produced it would not be possible to determine which took precedence. If any of their friends happened to be present when a need for this expression engrossed their hostesses, the friends were invited to go home because, as A expostulated when a conspicuous lack of hospitality was called to her attention, "they never get the words right but they won't keep still." Quite possibly the words their guests knew were the conventionally "right" ones.

Neither their religious nor their secular repertoire included rare musical items. The exceptional factor was in the rendering of the text, but any attempt to bring their version into line with what the lyricist had intended was rejected with vehemence. At the time I was recapturing, their favorite selections were "Home on the Range," "The Isle of Capri" and, in the category of sacred music, "Onward, Christian Soldiers." These were delivered in a vigorous tempo without modulation of either voice or tramping feet. The playroom was directly above the entrance hall in our house outside Philadelphia. The favorite time for the musical program was late afternoon, just before baths and supper. A guest coming for tea invariably stopped short immediately over the threshold to look with startled apprehension at the ceiling, and the chandelier swinging from it. We were unable, of course, to have any conversation until we had got out of the hall and into the living room.

Sometimes, however, a guest would pause in the hall, in shock perhaps, or possibly to identify with a familiar tune the words. Had I been able to make myself heard I could have explained their marching step that brought the knee not quite to the chin. This gave greater driving power to the downstamp. That the words could be heard clearly above this is an indication of the carrying quality of their voices. I found some comfort, I needed to find some, in their ability to sing in key and on pitch.

In "The Isle of Capri," their only deviation from the text was in the title—"The Vile of Kupree," they enunciated piercingly, and swept into action. They might have developed other interpretations to their liking, given sufficient opportunities for practice; these I had curtailed by a ruling. I had not considered my ruling unfair nor my nervous system unnaturally fragile but at the end of one week of "The Vile of Kupree" I imposed a limit. Each twin could sing it ten times a day, no more. A tells me it was only five times apiece and still feels I was churlish. I maintain either figure was a generous allotment. Heard twenty times in one day, or even ten, any song frays the ear and nervous system.

The treatment of "Home on the Range" included wider variations. These were not developed; they sprang full-panoplied. At the first performance to which I was an invited audience, the announcement of the selection was "Home by the Range." Each syllable thereafter was as clearly articulated as those of the title.

"Oh, there never was heard a scourging word where the deer and the amblions grow."

These words evoked for me a misty, pastoral atmosphere. I did not ask what they conveyed to A and B.

The one interpretation I attempted to modify, tactfully, I

thought, was of "Onward, Christian Soldiers." The anachronism introduced, though startling to hear, was entirely plausible to them. I should have realized this when I heard it since I had been told that at Sunday school, asked if anyone could tell what Jesus did when He grew up, B had said decisively:

"I expect he worked at the typewriter like my mommy."

Therefore, after they had sung "On a Christian soldier, marching to the wars, with a cross of Jesus going on by fours," they moved into, for them, a consistent image. They sang "Christ, the royal master, leans against the phone."

This *dégagé* image of our Lord startled me into spontaneous interference. I repeated the words correctly and explained what they meant. When I had finished B said with lowering severity:

"Jesus likes our way better."

The day Grandfather and I sang in his automobile on the road from Anderson to Muncie, I think we said the words accurately, though the circumstances were unusual. I was the age of the twins at their hymn-singing peak; that may be why the memories returned together in spite of the gap of years between. I was the first grandchild and the only girl in the family. Perhaps it was the novelty of this after three sons that led Grandfather to choose me as a companion at such an early age I do not remember the first excursions.

Grandfather's factory was the Indiana Bridge Company in Muncie, Indiana, and he took me with him to see how constructions were coming along. We never sang on those trips. Grandfather would point out places along the way.

"That's so-and-so's farm," he would say, and tell me a story about it.

When he saw a farmer coming toward us driving a team,

he would stop the automobile at the side of the road so that the horses would not get frightened and bolt. Sometimes he got out and helped the farmer lead them past the machine.

We were not going to a bridge the day we sang. When I stormed that I could not climb around a bridge in a dress, why wasn't I wearing the usual bloomers, Mother said to stop shouting, I was not going to a bridge. I was going to Anderson to see Governor Durbin. Mother's explanation of what a governor was made no sense to me but since he was a friend of Grandfather's I would probably find him acceptable.

Anderson is twenty miles from Muncie and it was a hot day. We must have started at around the hottest part of it because it was after my nap that I stormed about the dress, which would make it around two o'clock. I had lunch, only we called it dinner, at twelve. The month was July, I know, because, passing fields, Grandfather would point and say with great satisfaction, "You see that? Right on schedule. Corn knee-high by the Fourth of July." Another saying I liked the picture of was "When oak leaves are the size of a squirrel's ear it's time to plant the corn."

When he drove the automobile Grandfather wore a long linen coat called a duster, cap and goggles. Grandmother made him wear them to keep the dust out of his clothes and his hair. The pair of goggles was the only part of the costume he said was necessary, but he wore it all. For the same reasons Mother had our seamstress make a coat for me too, and between them they had invented the most uncomfortable head covering I have ever owned, a sort of bonnet with an isinglass front so that I would not breathe in dust and get hay fever. The glass was ambered; everything I looked at was turned yellow. Inside it the sweat ran down my neck and glued my hair to the scalp. Also the sweat tickled, but

to scratch through the bonnet brought no relief, so I squirmed a good deal.

Grandfather was a patient man. Grandmother or Mother would have told me to stop fidgeting but he told me stories about his friend Governor Durbin, who worked very hard most of the year in Indianapolis. We were going to his farm. He could only come there in the summer when he was not so busy, since the legislature was not in session. These were familiar words to me but unpleasant. Grandfather was a state senator. Far too many times, in my opinion, when he had not come to see me or asked for me to be brought to his house I was told he was in Indianapolis, the legislature was in session. He had told me he did not like being in Indianapolis so much either but he had to be a senator because he wanted to get things better for men in prison and the way to do that was to get laws changed. These were phrases I used glibly. I had heard them so often I know now I put them to my own use. When I was disinclined to respond to a summons, I liked to say I could not because I was in session. Opposition to a pronouncement I voiced as "I am changing a law." I have no recollection of either of these pronouncements producing the effect I wanted.

We were talking about Indianapolis when we reached the Governor's farm. Indianapolis was a place I knew because my other grandparents lived there and I sometimes stayed with them.

My impression is of a long driveway from the road to the Governor's house but it could very well not have been. I have learned that distances and heights shrink astonishingly in the years between childhood and maturity. My memory, however, is clear and precise that we had just agreed Craig's candy store in Indianapolis had the best butterscotch drops in the world when Grandfather stopped the automobile and a man in a white suit came out on the porch to meet us. He started down the steps toward us but Grandfather waved him back.

"Wait till I get out of these dust catchers. I don't want to get a speck on that handsome ice cream suit of yours."

The mention of ice cream brought me out and on the driveway in a jiffy, peeling off my coat and my loathsome bonnet. My face and my hair were so wet underneath it, I wiped them with my arm and my hand two or three times. When we came up the steps and Grandfather said, "Emily, this is Governor Durbin," and I shook hands with him, my hand was sopping. He had to take a handkerchief out of the pocket of his coat to wipe off his own hands, but he was saying:

"I'm delighted to meet you, Emily. C.M., it was mighty good of you to drive down here on this hot day. It's a treat to see you."

"Treat" was a nice word, I thought, and hoped it would give the Governor an idea.

"Twenty miles and six-tenths," Grandfather was saying. "Engine ran like a hummingbird, but coming at that speed—we were hitting twenty-five pretty steadily—it does stir up the dust. I would appreciate a drink."

To Grandfather a drink meant exactly what it meant to me, a drink of water. I know now Grandfather had never tasted alcohol, because when he went into the Civil War at seventeen he had promised his father he would never drink so he no more knew the taste of alcohol than I knew it. The Governor said:

"C.M., I apologize for not having it right out here when you arrived. You certainly do want a drink, and here it comes."

The Governor's houseman had come through the screen

door—we never said "butler" in Indiana. He had on a white coat like the one Grandfather's houseman wore, he was colored, smiled warmly and carried a tray. There were two tall glasses on the tray filled with iced tea, I thought, with a fancy touch of sprigs of mint sticking around and above the top of the glass. I knew what mint looked like; we had a mint bed at our house, but we used it for mint sauce with lamb. I'd never seen it raw before with anything to drink, though I liked to eat it from the bed. The Governor said:

"Munroe, Senator Kimbrough has asked for a drink. That's a terrible thing to happen to people like you and me from Kentucky, isn't it?"

Munroe offered the tray to Grandfather. "I'm very sorry sir, but here you are and I'll get something right away for the little girl."

Grandfather took one of the glasses.

"Why, I wasn't expecting anything so special as this," he boomed. Grandfather's deep bass voice always boomed. "I was just looking forward to a glass of cold water after that dusty trip and don't fix anything for Emily. She and I will share this delicious concoction."

I was already reaching for the glass. Grandfather, bending down, put it in my hands.

"Hold it carefully," he said.

To my astonishment, the Governor and Munroe simultaneously jumped at me unmistakably as if they wanted to take the glass away. The Governor even said something like:

"Hold on there, C.M. Let Munroe get her a glass of milk or something. I don't think her mama would want her to have this."

If there was one abominable thing above all others to swallow, in my estimation it was milk. I spun around with my

40

back to the interferers and took a deep gulp from the glass. It choked me a little but I liked the taste. While Grandfather was explaining that Mother let me have iced tea once in a great while, this was a special occasion, I took some more swallows and then out of politeness turned around and gave the glass to Grandfather. He liked it too, said it was the best he'd ever tasted and quite different. The Governor and Munroe did not fuss any more about it. The Governor took the other glass, Munroe left, and Grandfather and I sat down side by side on a wicker settee that had a great many cushions, and hung by chains on either side from the ceiling. It was like one on Grandfather's porch at home and I indicated this was where I would like to be so that we could swing. While Grandfather and the Governor talked I pushed us back and forth—by sitting on the edge I could get one foot to the floor—and Grandfather and I finished the drink between us.

By and by the Governor asked if Grandfather would like another one. He did not say it in the way I was used to, like "Of course you will have," or "I insist," or "Do have another," but Grandfather accepted the offer enthusiastically. So did I, rejecting unequivocally suggestions of sarsaparilla or root beer. I did not take so much of the second one as I had taken of the first. I did not feel so thirsty and the swinging had made me a little dizzy so I stopped that too. The Governor said Munroe would take me to see a new calf and some baby pigs. I went with him but it was hot and I was still a little dizzy from the swing. When I told him Munroe said he wasn't surprised. He expected it was the swing that did it and brought me back to the house.

Grandfather and the Governor had gone indoors and were sitting at a big table in the library. They had a great many papers spread out on top of it and were so busy looking at

them and talking they did not notice me come in. I went over to a big chair in the corner. The chair had a wide enough seat for me to put my feet on and I rested my head on its arm. I do not think I went to sleep because I always resisted a nap, but when I saw Grandfather standing in front of the chair I was in and heard him say, "Why, here she is," I was surprised. He said we must be going, to say good-bye to the Governor. I shook hands with him and remembered to say thank you for a lovely time. He followed us to the top of the steps on the porch. He told me he was glad I had come and didn't like to see us go.

"C.M.," he asked, "are you sure you want to drive the machine back? Why don't you let my man take you and come home on the Interurban?"

Grandfather said he wouldn't hear of such a thing but he did let Munroe crank the automobile.

At the end of the driveway I looked back; that is why I remembered the driveway as long. The Governor and Munroe were still on the top step watching us. The breeze blew my hair all over my head and my face, and I loved it. I was not hot any more or dizzy. I suddenly remembered why I felt so good and so different and said it aloud.

"We didn't put our coats and hats on."

Grandfather took one hand off the wheel and slapped his leg.

"That's it," he said. "That's why I feel so fine. I was just thinking to myself that I don't know when I have felt so fine. I'm never going to wear those contraptions again. I wouldn't have believed they could make such a difference."

He began to sing, and I joined in his favorite hymn:

When He cometh, when He cometh to make up His jewels,
All the jewels, precious jewels, His loved and His own;
Like the stars of the morning, His bright crown adorning,
They shall shine in their beauty, bright gems for His crown.

He will gather, He will gather the gems for His kingdom,
All the pure ones, all the bright ones, His loved and His own.
Like the stars of the morning, His bright crown adorning,
They shall shine in their beauty, bright gems for His crown.

Little children, little children who love their Redeemer,
Are the jewels, precious jewels, His loved and His own.
Like the stars of the morning, His bright crown adorning,
They shall shine in their beauty, bright gems for His crown.

This was better than singing it around the piano on Sunday
night. We sang it loud into the breeze, all the verses, and
when we had finished we went back to the beginning and
sang it all over again at the top of our lungs. Then Grandfather said for some reason or other he felt a little tired. He
wasn't used to driving forty miles in one day. He thought
it might be a good idea to rest a little before we went on. He
pulled the machine to the side of the road, turned off the
engine, and we got out. We had stopped this side of a bank
soft and thick with grass and clover. There was a little brook
on the other side of it and I thought of taking off my socks
and shoes and wading but I was tired too from the driving
and singing. Grandfather took off the jacket of his suit, fold-
ing it up to make a pillow for his head, and lay down. I lay
down beside him and looked up at the sky. When I awoke
it was dusk and Grandfather was sitting up beside me.

"By Christopher," he was saying, "I must have dozed off.
We've got to be on our way or they'll be worried about us."

While he was cranking up I noticed I had grass stains on
my dress and knew that would not be well received but I did

not mention this when Grandfather got back into the automobile because I could see he was a little anxious. He climbed out again almost immediately.

"Forgot to light up," he explained. I followed him because I had always wanted to see the lamps lighted and had never been out late enough for it. There was one on each side of a grille. In the middle of this was his monogram that my father and two uncles had given him as a birthday present when he bought the Haines. It was very large and the letters CMK twined into one another. He unhooked and opened the glass front on each of the lamps. When he had lighted and turned them up just right the monogram glittered. I was admiring it and putting my hands across the lights to make shadows but Grandfather told me to hop back in.

"We'll have to skeedaddle" was what he said.

That is the last part of the ride I remember. The singing, the resting on the bank, lighting the lamps are sharp and clear. What happened after that I learned much later from Mother and my father.

They were waiting on the porch when we pulled up to the curb. They had been there a long time except for when they were in the house talking about telephoning Grandmother to find out if she had any news of us, and deciding if she had she would have telephoned them. They would make her anxious if they called her. Grandfather blew three times on the rubber bulb of the big horn that was just outside the door on his side where he could reach it. They hadn't needed that sound to tell them we were coming. They'd been watching up the street and seen the lamps two blocks away—in Indiana we called them squares. They had run down the steps, across the yard, down the other steps and across the sidewalk to the street, saying how glad they were to see us and were we all right. I had not answered. Grandfather told

45

them certainly everything was fine, they'd had a splendid day but that Emily was a little tired after a forty-mile drive and no wonder, so she was asleep. This was their first surprise because they had never known me to welcome sleep and certainly not without eating. The shock came when my father lifted me out and put me over his shoulder. He did not say anything until after they had watched Grandfather drive on to the corner to turn around. He always went to corners for this. I think he liked doing most things with a big sweep and he said himself he disliked reversing. They saw him on his way back up the street to his own house in the next square before they turned round to go into ours. That was when my father said:

"Girl"—this was his special name for Mother—"go around behind me and smell Emily."

Mother, telling me about it, said she hoped never again so long as she lived to have such doubts of my father's sanity and certainly she would never again know such disbelief as when she had done what he had asked.

"Hal," she had told him, and could not get her voice above a cracked whisper, "she smells of whiskey."

Mother said if ever people looked at each other with a wild surmise, she and my father were the most wildly surmising. When the shock abated enough for them to move, my father carried me to my bed while Mother telephoned Dr. Cowing. I was undressed, in bed, a parent on either side of me, when the doctor arrived. The only signs of life I'd given other than my heart beating, Mother told him, were unintelligible murmurs and a snatch of what sounded like a familiar hymn.

Dr. Cowing corroborated their diagnosis but soothed their wild alarm.

46

"Yes," he had said, "Emily is drunk but not dead, and not likely to die. She'll be fit as a fiddle tomorrow morning. Just let her sleep it off. I doubt that she'll even have a headache."

As he left, she said, he called back:

"If you find out where she got it I'd be interested to know. Just in case," he added, "I have other patients with the same complaint." He was going down the steps.

"She's been with her grandfather all afternoon. They drove to Anderson in the Haines," my father told him.

Mother said Dr. Cowing stopped and turned around so abruptly he nearly fell off the bottom step.

"With C.M.? Why, he's never had a drop to drink in his life. I know that for a fact."

As if, Mother always emphasized in the story, this was news to her and Grandfather's son.

"Why, he'd as soon let Emily have rat poison. Where on earth did he take her that she could have got at it?"

"They went to see the Governor," my father told him, and Mother always asserted it was the first time she'd ever seen anybody's eyes actually bulge. If he said anything Mother and my father did not remember it but when Daddy told the story he said the doctor just stood there shaking his head hard like a man with a fly buzzing around it.

They did not go back into the house until the doctor had driven away. They watched him unhook from the horse's bridle the iron weight that hitched her, put it back in the buggy and climb in. They still hoped, Daddy said, he might have some suggestion. He did, just as he was slapping the reins over his horse to start moving.

"Suppose I drop by and talk to C.M.," was his suggestion. Daddy called after him.

"Better not. Leave it alone."

47

Mother said this was typical of Dr. Cowing, a last conversation between the front porch and the buggy. He would call back instructions when he had got all the way down to the corner, leaning way out and cupping a hand to his mouth. His patients always waited on the porch no matter what the weather until he was out of earshot because he always had final instructions after he had started and sometimes they were the most important.

"Beat up an egg in some milk, nutmeg on top; nourishing," he would call back, or "Sweet spirits of nitre; bring down the fever." This time it was "She may need calomel tomorrow; liver."

They went back into the house and Daddy telephoned Grandmother. Mother did not want her alarmed, but Daddy thought he might get some notion of when I might have wandered off by myself where I could have got hold of the whiskey, though he promised Mother he wouldn't mention that. She stood beside him in the back hall where the telephone was, on the wall. When he had hung up and turned back to her, she said he looked as if he had had a shock, and he had.

"My father," he told her, "has gone to bed without any supper and left his clothes in the middle of the floor in his bedroom. Mother says he has never done such a thing before. She says it just goes to show he had no business driving all that way on a hot day. It wore him out."

Mother said she and Daddy stood there in the hall and for the first time since the whole thing began they grinned at each other.

"Your father," Mother told him redundantly, "has had some whiskey."

"Mother says," Daddy added, "the Governor called up to

48

know if Father had got home all right. She thought that was very thoughtful of him but it annoyed her a little. Much as she hates that automobile, she didn't care to have anyone imply Father isn't a skillful driver."

They were still talking it over when they went to bed after another look at me. Mother said I seemed like a cherub until she bent down to kiss me.

The next morning I was evidently fully recovered because I did not have to take calomel. I would have remembered that because of all abominations this was the one I detested most.

Mother did not ask me anything about the visit to Anderson and evidently I had not thought any part of it exceptional because I said only that we'd had a very nice time. Having found out that Grandfather, like me, was in splendid health the next day, my parents did not take up the subject with him. Certainly it was not one about which they wished to speculate among their friends, so the source of my downfall and Grandfather's would have remained a secret, but Grandmother innocently gave it away.

One morning about a week after our excursion she telephoned Mother. They talked or saw each other nearly every day but there was urgency in this call.

"Lottie," she said, "I wish you'd come over. I need your help." Mother said she'd dropped whatever she was doing and had gone immediately.

Grandmother took her straight to the kitchen. Erna, the cook, was stirring something in a pitcher on the sink.

"It's iced tea"—Grandmother fairly spat out the words—"and it's driving us crazy. For a week Charles has been asking every day for iced tea and when we give it to him it isn't the way he wants it."

Mother said Erna poured something into the pitcher and began pounding it as if she were making butter, and she was angry.

"Fifteen years I've been here and he's never fancied iced tea. Now it's all he wants and I can't make it to suit him. Says it's got to have a special mint flavor. I put mint on the outside and now I'm going to put it on the inside and he won't be satisfied."

Then Grandmother took up the complaint and Mother said it was a lightning flash that broke through the clouds.

"The Governor gave it to him that day he went to Anderson," she said. "Charles never fancied iced tea before; and now he says he didn't know how good it could be. It had mint, was all he could tell us, with a special flavor that was the best thing he'd ever tasted. He can't stop talking about it."

It was Erna's turn again.

"I put more sugar in, he says it's too sweet. I put less, it's bitter. Now I've boiled up some mint; I'll try that. He won't like it," she added. When she spoke again her teeth were closed. "So I says, 'Call up Mrs. Hal. She comes from Indianapolis. Maybe they know some kind of fancy tea-making I ain't heard tell of.'"

Grandmother looked appealingly at Mother.

"If you don't know any, Lottie, I'm going to call the Governor and get the recipe direct from him."

Mother said she felt as if the lightning had struck her. She actually leaned against the sink to steady herself, praying for something she could say that would divert that telephone call. Her prayer was answered and she would say, always raising her head at that point with an amused and deliberate arrogance:

"I may not be able to cook but I could have been a diplomat." This is what she told Grandmother:

"You know, I don't believe I would telephone or write to the Governor for that recipe. You see, he comes originally from Kentucky. Southerners have recipes that are handed down from generation to generation and kept in the family. Another Southerner would never ask such a secret to be given away. If you should ask, he'd realize you didn't know this tradition, not being a Southerner, and being a Southern gentleman he would really be distressed. He'd want on one hand to oblige you but on the other hand would be honor bound to keep a family tradition."

Grandmother accepted this and thanked Mother.

"I wouldn't have known that," she said, "and I certainly wouldn't embarrass him. He was showing his Southern hospitality by giving the best he had. Charles will just have to make do with what we offer him."

Erna was still pounding in the pitcher when Mother left. Grandfather lost his taste for iced tea. By the end of the summer Erna had stopped making it. Every Sunday night after supper at Grandfather's house we all sang "When He Cometh, When He Cometh," but I do not remember singing it another time in the automobile.

IV

Name-Calling

My stepmother, moving this winter from the apartment in which she has lived since my father's death, asked me to help her sort out and decide what things could be disposed of. At the bookshelves, making two piles, one to give to the hospital, the other to pack, I dropped a volume because of the shock the words of the title transmitted. The secret companion of my childhood lay dead at my feet. For years she had been my dearest friend, but sometime in my growing up she had gone away and I had forgotten about her. I had created her and now because my reading and I were older, I had killed her. I know exactly where on the shelves at our house in Muncie that book and its companion volume had stood, at just the right height for me to read and to reach; but I never took either volume from the shelf. Their title, *Abbeys, Castles and Ancient Halls in England, Scotland and Wales,* gave me my friend and wide travels.

From the moment I was in bed until sleep took me from her, I was Abbey's guest at one of her Castles or Ancient Halls. We arrived together, each on a milk-white steed.

Trumpets blew from the ramparts, pennants were unfurled, a drawbridge was lowered, and we clattered across it into the great banquet hall, to the resounding cheers of the loyal serfs. There we dined, I expect, on creamed chicken, mashed potatoes with gravy, peas, vanilla ice cream with chocolate sauce and angel food cake, the menu for gala occasions with which I was familiar. As a landowner, Abbey made the dukes of England seem property owners in Levittown. We seldom visited twice one of her castles or ancient halls. When our prancing steeds were brought to us, we made a choice, amicably, and on the instant plunged full gallop toward England, Scotland or Wales.

The death of Abbey made me remember how important names have always been to me. I accepted friendship readily, even promoted it with someone whose name I liked. I had never known anyone called Abbie, I doubt that I had heard the word pronounced; but seeing it on the title, I was immediately drawn to a friendship with that girl. I choose to believe incidental the material advantages this friendship offered.

Though I did not know any Josephines, I disliked the name venomously. The Christmas I was six years old, Grandmother Wiles gave me a doll whose clothes had been made by Grandmother's dressmaker in Indianapolis. Every garment from panties to pink-silk-covered-with-net dress was stitched to its body. Each time a visitor came to call on Grandmother, staying with us in Muncie for the holidays, she would ask to see the doll with the exquisite clothes she had heard so much about. I would stand by while they exclaimed over the real lace edging of the petticoats and the fine sewing, "every stitch by hand." Asked what I called this beautiful doll, I would answer, "Josephine."

When I was twelve years old, we lived in Chicago and I went to Miss Faulkner's School. Josephine Root came into our class the middle of the first term and was assigned a seat next to mine. At recess, I told my friends she smelled because that was the worst thing I could think of to say about her. She was bright, gentle and sweet as a rose, and we became friends but not chums. I always felt shy with her. I have never known another Josephine.

"Hector," spoken aloud, marked a day on my calendar to be remembered with joy and a special thank you in my prayers. Whatever their other connotations, Christmas on my calendar was for presents, Valentine's Day, of course, for valentines, Easter, eggs and rabbits, Halloween, dressing up and scaring people, Thanksgiving, turkey and pumpkin pie, and Hector's Day, my first dog. I had begged for one, prayed, made wishes on white horses and the first star, but my father, usually reasonable, had been a man of stone against every pleading argument.

"It always ends in a heartbreak," he had said to Mother, in my hearing. Since my conviction was that my heart would break if I did not own a dog, I could only believe his mind was so addled, my reasonable arguments had not got through to him. The day, glorious day forever marked on my calendar, when his mind cleared, I had heard him say to Mother:

"I haven't heard that since Hector was a pup."

There was my opening and I plunged through it, weeping, pleading, stamping. If my father had had a puppy named Hector, how could he deny me one, how could he let me be the only person in the world who did not have a puppy? If my parents attempted an explanation or a justification, I did not hear it, and suddenly they capitulated. Hector, Saint Hector, had interceded for me.

The line of dogs that came into my possession after that was long but not distinguished. I think only the first one was purchased. After that I gathered them in wherever I found them. Frequently I had to return one with apology to its rightful and distraught owner, but I was philosophical about these transients, confident that I would shortly garner a replacement. I never called one Hector. I think I felt it would be disrespectful to someone I mentioned in my prayers, and the only name I remember until much later years and dogs was the one I gave my first, a cocker spaniel puppy. Actually I gave him two names because they were in stories I had read and I could not decide between them. I added a third because it did not occur to me anyone could be without a last name. I neither used nor permitted an abridgment either when speaking of him or summoning, "Here, White Socks Merry Legs Kimbrough."

Mother's name was Charlotte Emily. She grew up in a family and time of name diminutives. She was the only child of my grandfather's second marriage. Her predecessors by his first wife were called Freddie, Addie and Lulie, and she became Lottie. I do not know for whom she was named. Her mother, my grandmother, was Sarah Jane. Another Sarah might have become Sally but not Grandmother Wiles. I cannot imagine that stately, rigidly corseted figure permitting any trifling with her name at any age. She bore him a child but I never heard her speak of or to her husband except as Mr. Wiles. Mother's figure was slight. Except during pregnancy it never carried more than ninety-eight pounds. She stood, without whalebones, as straight as her mother. All fire and spirit in her enthusiasms and her dislikes, she abominated the name Lottie so much, this disfavor embraced all diminutives. She protested my being named for her and yielded to my father's insistence only if the Charlotte was dropped and no middle name substituted.

"Just Emily," she said. "You can't make an *ie* ending out of that."

It evidently did not occur to her I might have become an Emmy with a *y*, and I did not. I never had a nickname and I always wanted one. Margarets became Peggy, Elizabeths turned into Betty, Patricia was Patty, Frances was Franny, all with a *y*, but I was christened Emily and since, like being a ballet dancer, you have to start young to be nicknamed, I doubt that I will ever be Emmy.

Mother lost out in her insistence on a simple name and avoidance of nicknames when my brother was born. She had wanted to call him Wiles and my father had acquiesced happily, not only to please her but to avoid the continuation of his own. By the same plague that had afflicted Mother, my father had been stamped at his christening with a nickname. The friend honored by the christening was Harold.

"He was always called Hal," was Grandfather's defense of his son's name. "If we had named our boy Harold, which was, of course, our friend's actual name, we would have been temporizing." Grandfather Kimbrough never temporized, so my father was christened Hal.

The day after my brother was born, Grandfather and Grandmother Kimbrough came to our house to congratulate the parents of their first grandson and to meet the new arrival. In my opinion there was a great deal of silly fuss being made over this intruder into my nearly six years of undisputed sovereignty. I was expressing this opinion in the kitchen when I heard Grandfather's arrival. Even had I been sitting on the back fence—a favorite lookout—I would have heard it. Grandfather's voice in timbre was not unlike Chaliapin's; it had a carrying quality. There was a foot's difference of height in Chaliapin's favor but I think Grandfather's head was the more handsome. I had heard my Uncle Frank say that if his father's voice had been a football, Uncle Frank could have carried it from one goalpost to the other for a touchdown above any interference. It brought me on a run from the kitchen. Wherever Grandfather was, was exactly where I most wanted to be. He was in the vestibule. My father was helping him off with his overcoat; anyone would have known they were related, even though my father was slighter and his hair brown and curly; Grandfather's was white. Until I was fourteen or fifteen, I called my father Dada. After that I called him Daddy, because I thought it sounded more grown-up and stylish. Dada told me to help Grandfather take off his overshoes while he removed Grandmother's carriage boots. It was the twenty-second of December.

They sat side by side on a bench that was part of our hat-rack, with hooks on either side and a mirror behind them. The bench was really the lid of a holdall. Dada called it the junkyard. He would say:

"If you can find a ball in the junkyard, I'll play catch with you."

Dada was untying the ribbons that fastened Grandmother's carriage boots and I was pulling at Grandfather's overshoes when Grandfather said:

"Young Charles is a buster, I hear; ten pounds."

Dada stopped untying and looked up at Grandfather. I was surprised too. Grandmother turned toward him as much as she could on the narrow bench. She was just over five feet tall, with lively brown eyes, soft brown hair. (When she died at eighty-four, her hair was still brown.) Her displacement was modest. Grandfather was an expansive man. She spoke sharply.

"Lottie is calling the baby Wiles. I told you that, Charles."

Dada echoed:

"That's right, Father."

Grandfather beamed at them both, and down at me.

"Of course she's going to call him Wiles and so are all of you, but he's going to be Charles to me, Young Charles."

Dada and Grandmother exchanged a look; Dada went back to untying her carriage boots and I pulled off Grandfather's overshoes. We pried my grandparents off the bench and Dada took them to Mother and the baby's room. Mrs. Lothan came into our living room to meet them. She was the nurse who came where there was a new baby. When I went to a friend's house and Mrs. Lothan was there, I knew a baby was too.

Grandmother and Grandfather told her they were so glad to see her, and Grandfather added how much happier than the last one this time was. Grandmother said quickly:

"Hush, Charles, don't talk about that."

Grandfather went ahead with Mrs. Lothan. I heard Grandmother say to Dada, and she was shaking her head:

"I can't do a thing with your father, Hal."

And Dada laughed.

Years later when I was old enough to know what she meant, I remembered how often she would say to Mother:

"I've spent most of my married life, it seems to me, jerking at Charles' coat sleeve, and it hasn't done one mite of good."

She may have said it that morning, but what I remember is Dada smiling and asking her:

"Would you like to lay a bet that by the time we come back here, the baby will be named Charles?"

When she told him that mustn't happen, Dada told her he would be delighted if it did. They went out of the living room, not asking me if I wanted to go with them. Those days of my brother's arrival no one seemed to care whether I came or went, or noticed me at all. I was not supposed to be there anyway. Mother had told me I was going to visit Grandmother and Grandfather Wiles in Indianapolis. They would come over as usual for Christmas and I would go back with them. I was looking forward to that, but I had an ominous feeling this business of a baby's arriving had upset the schedule and was going to play havoc with my visit.

Grandmother and Grandfather Wiles, I'd heard, were coming over right away, three days ahead of Christmas, to see this baby, I supposed, and were going to stay at the big house with Grandmother and Grandfather Kimbrough instead of with us. No one had said whether I would go back with them or not go at all. It was my bitter contention, frequently and loudly expressed, that adults never stopped to explain anything fully. They were always going somewhere, dropping off bits and pieces of information as they hurried by.

It would be unrewarding, I decided, to resume the conversation in the kitchen the arrival of my grandparents had interrupted.

Even before the interruption, the conversation had not been to my liking. Conversations I enjoyed followed one of two patterns: a concentrated attention on what I was saying or full and explicit answers to questions I submitted. When other people did not live up to my standards, and this occurred frequently, I talked to myself. I enjoyed listening to my stories, but I was not always satisfied with the answers I gave to the questions I asked. Deciding to talk to myself, I sat on the floor in front of the fire, introducing a Socratic dialogue with:

"Why is no one paying any attention to me?"

Answer: "Because Christmas is coming in three days."

Question: "Is that why Lena does not want me in the kitchen?"

Answer: "Yes. She is cooking surprises."

Question: "Zoe is *my* nurse. Why does she tell Lena she can't wait to get her hands on that baby?"

Answer: "She was telling Lena what I am going to get for Christmas and changed the subject the way people do."

Question: "Why is Mother in bed?"

Answer: "Overtired. That's what everybody has been saying to her: 'Lottie, you mustn't get overtired.' Only, Dada calls her Girl."

Question: "Why does Dada call her Girl?"

Answer: "That is a silly question, because I've already asked Dada that and he told me. He said, 'Because she's my girl.' "

Question: "Why are Grandmother and Grandfather here to see this baby and not me?"

Answer: "Because it's new. They came to see our piano the day it was delivered."

Question: "Are people going to go on paying attention to this baby?"

Answer: "I don't know."

Question: "People say, 'Isn't it wonderful to have a brother?' Is it?"

Answer: "I don't know."

Question: "If they name him Wiles or Charles, what will you call him?"

Answer: "Brother."

The others were coming back. I heard them laughing. When they walked into the room, I saw Grandmother was shaking her head and she was not laughing; her mouth was tight. That meant she was not pleased, but Grandfather was in high old feather, as I'd heard said.

"Why, I never expected the baby to be named for me," he said. "I just told Lottie he would be Charles to *me*. It didn't take her a second to tell me that's what he would be for everybody, Charles Wiles."

"She took time to ask you why you hadn't named any of your own sons after you," Grandmother suggested. Grandfather spoke to Dada:

"I had no idea it would mean so much to me. I was a lot younger then, but, Hal," he added, "I don't want to overstep."

Dada patted his father's sleeve. "Listen, Father, Girl would do just about anything you asked, and we're keeping the Wiles, so Charles Wiles makes everybody happy. Emily, honey, aren't you forgetting something? Stand up for the grownups."

I stayed where I was and looked back in the fire. Dada was probably going to make me get up, but I heard Grandmother say, "No, Hal, leave her alone. It's a hard time for her, with her nose out of joint."

This was an appalling suggestion on top of everything else that had happened, but I would not give them the satisfaction of seeing me feel my nose for the damage.

They went past me into the vestibule. I think Dada was going to call me to help with the overshoes again because Grandmother said:

"No, Hal, I beg you, leave her alone."

Dada asked Mrs. Lothan to tell Lena he was going to the big house for dinner, he would be back early in the afternoon. While he was helping Grandfather put overshoes on, Grandmother came back into the living room to Mrs. Lothan. She wanted to be sure, she said, everything was all right. Was Dr. Cowing satisfied? Mrs. Lothan told her everything was just beautiful. Grandmother said:

"Two weeks early, and after the other terrible time we've been sick with worry. I'll call Mrs. Wiles again. She's nearly crazy with the trains not running on account of the snow, not even the Interurban; but they say the tracks will all be cleared by tomorrow."

Grandfather called and she hurried off.

Mrs. Lothan sat down on a chair, close to me by the fire, leaning past my shoulder to warm her hands.

"Emily," she told me, "don't be upset about what's going on around here. It will all settle down pretty soon, and you're going to love your brother and learn to help Zoe take care of him, but don't worry Mother and Dada. They're so happy."

This was the first time since she had come in the night, two days before, she had spoken to me more than a word or two. Her voice stirred a memory. I looked up at her.

"You've been here before, haven't you?"

She nodded. "I didn't think you'd remember. You were only four."

A picture was shaping.

"You brought another baby."

She nodded again. "Yes, I did." She shook her head, biting her lips. "That was a bad time."

The picture was growing clearer.

"I sat in the chair you're in. You put that baby on my lap. You let me hold it. You said it was only going to visit us for a little while."

She looked frightened and asked in only a whisper:

"You remember that?"

"You told me to hold out my arms. You put the baby there. You stood in front of me. You were just going to take it back. Something happened. Dada called you. You left it with me. You went away. You were running."

Bit by bit, I was piecing it together.

"I held the baby a long, long time. You came back. My arms were asleep but I held on. You said I was a fine nurse. Then you took the baby away. I never saw it any more. What happened to it?"

Mrs. Lothan got up from her chair.

"She went away. I wanted you to hold her before she went. I didn't mean it to be so long. Your mother needed me. I had to go."

She smiled down at me. "I have to go now. That fat brother of yours wants to be fed. I can hear him. But everything's just fine."

Her stiff skirt made a pleasant noise when she hurried. That and her voice were what had brought back the other time. Something made me sure that if I stayed exactly where I was, keeping as still as "Still Pond, No More Moving," but remembering hard, the whole of that other time would come to me. It did come and it is as clear today as on that December morning in front of the fire. My mother and father never knew I had sat there with a baby, never knew what I had heard.

Mother had called out in a high voice:

"Was there no one to speak for her? All strangers."

Dada's voice was rusty like someone with a cold:

"Girl, Girl, listen to me. I would have lost *you*." And Mother's voice over his:

"A stranger, a stranger. And no one to speak for her. She is Ruth, Ruth, Ruth." Over and over and over she said it:

"She is Ruth, Ruth the stranger, Ruth, Ruth."

That day I was taken away to Grandmother and Grandfather Wiles' in Indianapolis. When I came back after quite a long visit, Mother and Dada had been on a trip. Everyone was happy at being home together again. If I asked where that baby was I had seen for a few minutes, I do not remember.

The headstone in the family plot at Muncie reads:
Ruth Kimbrough.

V

Improbabilities

One day this summer during lunch, we exchanged anecdotes about improbable personal happenings. There were four at the table—Cornelia, Sophy, Alice and I. My friendship with Cornelia and Sophy began during our schooldays. No one of us wishes to be more specific than that about the length of time this has covered. The last few summers we have rented a house together in Rhode Island. Alice was our guest. Her physical proportions are diminutive, her spirit and convictions of Herculean proportions. She exercises these as a distinguished member of an international organization. The improbable occurrence she told us about had come upon her in Teheran, where she had gone for a meeting of this organization. Arriving, she had learned, to her discomfiture, she was to stay at a hotel located on the outskirts of the city, chosen because it provided a more pleasant environment than the congested midtown area. Certainly the happiest choice, she assured us, had she been there for pleasure, but since all the sessions were held midtown and the social occasions immediately following were also in the heart of the city, it was hard to accommodate to the schedule the distance to be traveled for changes of clothes.

"It really doesn't take a long time for me to dress," she interpolated apologetically and unnecessarily, because we know the tempo she follows makes her always the first among us to be ready for any occasion. Over the eighty-odd years of her life her pace seems to have accelerated.

On the day in Teheran this preposterous thing happened, she said, there had been very little time in the schedule between the closing of the afternoon session and a state dinner. Even for those lodging in the city it was tight planning but for her on the outskirts it was more nearly a marathon test. She had come out of the meeting at a trot, and with luck found a taxi immediately, given the name of her hotel and indicated in pantomime the driver must hurry. There was no common language to share; she had tried every one she knew. The driver had set off at the usual man-, child- and animal-slaughtering pace customary in that area. She had learned a request by any method to drive more carefully was incomprehensible, so she had closed her eyes.

"I opened them suddenly, dreading what might be under the wheel because the car had stopped, though I'd felt no bump. The driver was getting out, and I indicated my anxiety. He understood, shook his head and smiled reassuringly. Then he patted his stomach and pointed to a café on the other side of the road. I watched him cross over, select a table, seat himself at it and pick up a menu. I called out to him in fury; he waved a reassuring hand. A waiter came and took his order, returned after some little time with enough dishes to provide a full meal and, at a request, came a second time with a small bottle of wine. The food was eaten, the wine drunk with the leisure of enjoyment. The check was called for, paid and after a last tipping of the wine bottle to make sure no drops remained, my chauffeur rose from the table, selected a toothpick from the container there, and employing it, sauntered back across the road. Reaching his car he flung the toothpick away, leapt into his seat, turned to smile at me and resumed his pursuit of whatever game could be run down."

Savoring every aspect of the episode—Alice's fury and helplessness, the driver's bland indifference, the incredibility of such a performance—Cornelia said ruefully, "Isn't it maddening you could never put that in a story?"

Alice was obviously surprised. "But it *is* a story," she countered. "I don't know what you mean."

Explaining, we talked over one another.

"If you were writing a story that involved your being late to the dinner and gave this as a reason, no reader would believe it. You'd have to invent something more prosaic, much less colorful. Every writer dreads the accusation of an incident being 'contrived.' Even if you're doing a straight chronicle of, say, a trip, you have to understate things that have happened in order to *make* them credible. You're always discarding something you really want to put into a story because it's too much, it won't go over."

Alice broke through the babel. She was nodding her head.

"Well, that explains something I've never really understood. Years ago I was on a ship with Katharine Cornell and Guthrie McClintic and I happened to be standing beside them when we came into the Bay of Naples. It was sunset. There were boats with red sails reflected in the water. I was nearly speechless over the beauty of it, but I did say to Mr. McClintic, 'What a setting in a play that would make,' and do you know what he said?"

Cornelia, wise in the theater, smiled. "I can guess."

70

"He said," Alice continued, " 'No, you could never use it. It's too much.' So that's what he meant."

"It's like the well-known long arm of coincidence," I said. "It happens to everybody, but you can't make it believable in writing." Over a chorus of agreement, and Alice's look of puzzlement, I developed my assertion. Here's an example, a story my stepmother tells: The summer she was eighteen, she and her cousin Pauline, the same age, went with their respective mothers to Venice. When she was born, Pauline's father had begun a string of pearls to be given her on her eighteenth birthday. The pearls were graduated in size to a large center one. She was wearing the necklace on a morning when the two girls went to the American Express office that is on Saint Mark's Square. As they were crossing the square on their way back to the hotel, Pauline stopped abruptly, cupping her hand over her chest. She was trembling, my stepmother said, and so frightened she could scarcely speak, except in a kind of croaking: "My pearls." Evidently, in those days pearls were not strung with knots between, so they had scattered. Pauline was sure it had happened at that moment so they were careful not to move from the spot as they gathered up, they hoped, all of them. They were still only a few yards from the American Express office so they turned back, put the pearls on a table there and counted them. They found all but the center one, the biggest. Pauline tied the others into a handkerchief, put it in her bag and they started again for the hotel, Pauline in tears now, saying over and over she could never tell her father, all those years he had spent collecting the pearls, especially the big one, what could she do?

Every tourist to Venice knows the thousands of pigeons that meet in Saint Mark's Square and the vendors of little paper cornucopias that hold a kind of white bean pigeons seem to like. Tourists buy the beans, pigeons perch on the head, the shoulders, the hands of the feeder and the enterprising bean vendor, with a camera handy, makes postcard snapshots the tourist happily distributes to his family, friends and memory book. Fighting among themselves, the pigeons frequently drop the bean and swoop down to retrieve it from the pavement. A pigeon swooped down for one at my stepmother's feet. She will never know what made her say "Shoo" to that bird among the thousands and pick up the bean it dropped. The bean was that pearl, the biggest of all. "Just try putting that in a story," I ended.

"Cornelia and Sophy can verify most of this one," I told Alice. Overriding their suggestions that I had told enough, I gave her another improbability.

Cornelia and I were bridesmaids in Sophy's wedding, in Devon, Pennsylvania. Cornelia and her family had recently moved from Bryn Mawr to New York and I was to stay with them there after the wedding. Mrs. Skinner had come over for the wedding and was staying on a few days with friends. Cornelia was making her Broadway debut in *Blood and Sand,* in which her father, Otis Skinner, was the star. Sophy had moved the day of her wedding from Saturday to Friday so that Cornelia could be a bridesmaid, since certainly the actress could not miss a performance. Nevertheless she had to leave early and as she got up from the bridal table, I realized I did not know the New York address. She called it back to me and the usher sitting at my right wrote it down on my place card and I tucked it into my bag. Some hours later, arriving in New York, I went by taxi to the address the usher had written. I had expected to tell a doorman which apartment I was visiting, but a maid came across the sidewalk as I was paying the driver. She said:

"We're expecting you, miss, but you'll have to come round by the back way for they're painting the front. I'll show you."

She took my bags and I followed her up a back stairway. She led me into a bedroom, put one bag on a luggage rack and opened it. Those were the days when bags included monogrammed fittings in the lid. It must have been the sight of these and the initials on them that caused her to start suddenly, turn on the overhead light and look at me closely.

"Oh, miss," she said. Her voice quavered and she looked agitated. "Are you coming here?"

This, I thought, was an odd question, and I answered it with some indignation:

"Of course I'm coming here."

Then I felt in my stomach bewildered misgivings.

"Isn't this Mr. Otis Skinner's apartment?" I asked.

"Oh, no, miss, this is Mr. Morgan's *house*."

Perhaps I waited a second for this information to penetrate my confusion. My recollection is that I jumped past her, slammed down the lid of the bag, snatched it up, ran from the room down the stairs and out into the street again. If she said anything or followed me, I did not know it in my panic to get out, and I did not stop running until I was on the sidewalk, facing a policeman.

"Anything the matter, miss?" he asked.

"This is the wrong house," I told him. "I'm looking for Mr. Otis Skinner's. I must have got the number wrong," and I thought balefully of that usher. Excitement and maybe champagne had obviously addled him and I hoped he would end in a drunkard's grave.

"Well," the policeman said, "I don't believe you're so far off. There's a Mr. Skinner on my beat, just around the corner. Give me your bag and we'll go round there."

He rang the doorbell of the house he knew and after a long time and a second ring, it was opened by what I then considered an old gentleman (he was probably fifty or a little under), wearing over pajamas a handsome brocade dressing gown. One look at him and I knew panic.

"Oh," I wailed, "you're not the right Mr. Skinner," and was on the run again. Perhaps the policeman stayed to apologize. He had not caught up with me when I reached the corner simultaneously with a cruising taxi I hailed and flung myself into. The driver asked me where I wanted to go; I realized I did not know. It would not have occurred to me to go by myself to a hotel and I could not think of friends I could telephone at that hour, waking their families as I had wakened the wrong Mr. Skinner. I did not know where to find a telephone, so I told the whole story to the taxi driver. Telling it, I had a brilliant solution. He could take me back to the Pennsylvania Station, I told him. I would get the midnight train to Philadelphia. I had done that many a time before when a group of us from college had come over to see a play. Then I would get a train back to New York. A train was the safest place and I would ride back and forth until it was not too early in the morning to telephone someone in Philadelphia or New York, whichever place I happened to be.

"Well, before you do that," the driver suggested, "I've got an idea that just come to me. I know a stagehand at the theater where your Mr. Skinner is at. Maybe he hasn't quit work yet and maybe he'll know where that Mr. Skinner lives or know how to find out."

Thankfully, I agreed.

The front of the theater was dark, of course, but as the driver was telling me he would hunt around for an alley to

the back, the door to the street opened and Mr. Skinner came out. Mr. Skinner later said he was thankful no enterprising press agent was in the vicinity to see a girl rush at him from a taxi, fling her arms around his neck and burst into sobs, saying over and over:

"Oh, thank God, I've found you at last."

It was the one night in the whole run of the play, he also said later, he had stayed after its closing because a friend catching a late train had come to his dressing room for a chat and there was no time to go elsewhere.

By the time we reached home (the right address had one difference in numerals that spanned some thirty-odd blocks), I was serene again, thoroughly enjoying myself. We found Cornelia giving an excellent performance of every tragedy queen, pacing the floor wringing her hands. She had come home from the play, worried a little, and after an hour spread her alarm. She had telephoned her mother in Philadelphia; her mother had telephoned Sophy's poor family, asleep at last after the long wedding day and the departure of the last guest. No, I had not stayed the night with them. They had seen me off, but certainly they would start making inquiries, poor souls. We called them immediately the reassuring news that I had arrived. Their voices when I spoke to them had not the warmth I had always known. I was even cut off in the middle of telling everything that had happened to me.

Some months later Mrs. Skinner wrote me a letter:

"I must tell you something that happened to me yesterday at a tea party. A very distinguished-looking gentleman came up and asked if I was Mrs. Otis Skinner. He said he had had a disheartening experience a few months before when in the middle of the night his doorbell had rung and he had opened the door to a policeman and a young girl in obvious distress. At the sight of him her distress had become greater. She had said, 'Oh, you're not the right Mr. Skinner,' and run away. Very disturbing and unflattering. The policeman who had brought her to me told me she was looking for Mr. Otis Skinner and I realized what an inferior brand mine is, as I am, alas, only a satin Skinner—you know, Emily, the Skinner satins?"

Several years later, at a party one night, someone asked me to tell the story of that night in New York. When I had finished, one of the guests was looking at me round-eyed and with more breathless interest than it seemed to me the story warranted. She barely let me finish the coincidence of the Mr. Satin Skinner. She was calling to her hostess across the room from us:

"You remember when Miss Kimbrough came in tonight, I thought she was Mary Smith?" (I don't remember the actual name.) She turned back to me.

"Mary Smith is an old friend of mine and I know another side of your story that really ties it up. It used to be a favorite dinner-table conversation piece in her family, everybody giving his solution of the mystery."

She included the group in her explanation. "Mary is a cousin of the Morgans. She lives on Long Island. She had been abroad with her family for the summer but had come back ahead of them to look for a job in New York. She had graduated from college in June—" "Just like me," I interjected, stressing the likeness between us because I was so fascinated with this story. The guest nodded and continued:

"The house in town had not been opened. The family was still in the country and some painting and redecorating was being done. But there was a maid there, a comparatively new one, at least she had never seen Mary. The maid, Irish and excitable, was told to expect the arrival of a family relative, have a room ready for her. She did what she was told but when she opened the suitcase of the visitor she saw initials that did not match the name she was expecting and had carefully memorized. When she asked the young lady if there was some mistake, she had been frightened out of her life by the young lady's actions, jumping past her, slamming down the lid of the suitcase, grabbing up her coat and running like someone possessed all the way down and out into the street before a body could stop her, 'Like she was a burglar, surprised in her wicked work'—I can quote verbatim, I've heard it so many times. There was no trace of the intruder, though the maid had opened the front door and peeked out, so maybe she was in the house, hiding somewhere. The maid, scared to death every step of the way, had found the night watchman down in the basement, and together they'd searched the house. Not a trace could they find. Together they decided the family ought to be warned about this and had telephoned to Long Island. The family did take it seriously enough to notify the police, ask them to keep a special watch on the house. The favorite theory was that the girl visitor was the tool of a gang of burglars. They'd used her likeness to my friend— her picture was pretty frequently in stylish magazines—to get her into the house, knowing it was closed and the family away. Once there, she was to case the joint and bring back to the gang the layout of the upper floors." She turned back to me. "I want to bring you and Mary together so you can see for yourself. What a table conversation piece this is going to make when I tell her family!"

Mary and I have never met and I have not been in Mr. Morgan's house again.

The day after these table conversation pieces, Ellen Garrison came to spend the night with us. Though any time with Ellen is unmitigated delight, over the telephone I had urged her not to come because the day before, a hurricane had roared through their countryside and ours and I had been hearing on the radio about the roads that were blocked by fallen trees, and flooding. Ellen said in their immediate area the storm had been a tornado; she and Lloyd, her husband, standing at the window, had watched it come, a whirling black mass that went over them in less than a minute and left over a hundred trees on their own place uprooted, a heartbreaking thing to see, and their road impassable. But the county team had worked all night, the road was cleared, and certainly she was coming. Since Ellen has been a very dear friend since our classmate days at college, I have reason and precedent to know she carries out whatever plans she has set down; her scant hundred pounds are welded by her determination into a dynamo of energy.

She arrived jubilant with triumph that though she'd had to go thirty miles out of her way, she had made up the time by driving at 80 and had fortified herself by eating, as she drove, a sandwich she'd brought with her.

We waited to ask her about the storm and the roads until we had eaten dinner and were relaxed around a fire. Though we had been swimming in the morning, the evening had turned chilly. The storm, she repeated, had been a tornado but not a twister. She had this information from the weather bureau. Ellen likes accuracy and detail and tends to emphasize both. The tornado had come and gone so fast it allowed no time, watching it, to be frightened. It would take weeks to clear the place of the fallen trees. She was glad to get away for a little while from the sight of those uprooted, dying live things. Once she'd detoured from that immediate area the drive over to us had been by the way she'd always come; the highways were clear. When I reminded her she said she'd gone thirty miles out of her way, she admitted with some embarrassment that had been her fault, not the storm's; she'd missed the turnoff. "I think I was looking for my sandwich. But when I found what I had done," she added, and grinned sheepishly, "I was so desperate that I'd be late, I very nearly offered a propitiation, only a piece of sandwich did not seem quite appropriate."

For all her insistence on the specific, Ellen can be obscure. Catching the looks exchanged among the others of us that indicated lack of enlightenment, "I didn't tell you about that time on the dreadful road in Greece. Well, I'd better tell you so you'll know what I meant," and she began her story.

"It was, of course, just coincidence but so extraordinary you would never have believed it if you had read it in a book."

She interrupted herself to ask why I looked so startled and had made a funny noise. "I haven't even told you yet what happened." I urged her for heaven's sake to go on with the story; I would tell her later. Watching me a little doubtfully, she did continue.

"It happened during a cruise we took in Greece on the Stephen Curriers' boat, a lovely congenial group of ten, five couples. We had put into Leonidion, a little harbor on the coast of the Peloponnesus, south of Nauplia, and we had to be in Nauplia in two days because one couple, the Woffords, had to leave us there to get back to Athens for their flight home. However, we had a day between, and Stephen suggested that instead of spending it in Nauplia, a place we knew quite well, we might get a car and drive to Sparta, which we'd never seen. Stephen and Lloyd worked it out on the map and it looked very easy. The Woffords decided not to come because they had packing to do and letters to write. So eight of us left the boat; we would be back in plenty of time for a farewell dinner on board.

"In Leonidion the men scattered to round up two cars and drivers. We'd done the same kind of day trip several times on the cruise and never had any trouble getting cars and drivers. There was always someone right on the dock who would tell us where to go, or lead us, or had a car himself and a relative who also had one. Here there didn't seem to be any cars or relatives. Finally the men rounded up two ancient vehicles with drivers; Lloyd and Stephen showed them Sparta on the map, and the spot where we were. Could they take us there? Was it a good road?

"With a great deal of talk, of which we understood one or two words, and swaggering pantomime, they gave us an assurance that no one in all Greece knew so well the way to Sparta, and the way was beautiful. So we got into the two cars, the women in one, the men in the lead. I don't know why we divided up that way, but that's how we started off.

"After a very short distance it was evident to all of us in the second car that neither driver had the faintest idea how to get to Sparta. The road was certainly not a highway; it looked and felt as if it were used only for goats to travel. Whenever we came to a farmhouse, and this was not very often, or saw a shepherd in a field, both drivers would leave the cars and have a long talk, come back nodding to us and to each other that certainly they were right and we were on the road they knew so well. Then they would stop again at the next person they saw. Our impression was the people they talked to had never heard of Sparta. The so-called road climbed and climbed up a mountain we later found out was Mount Hagios Elias, and the higher we went, the deeper the ruts. We came out on a great wide plateau and there we got totally lost. We even lost the road, such as it was. Then the rains came, and we crawled, slithering and jouncing. A little brook crossed the plain, and that's where we stuck when we tried to cross it."

Ellen stopped, looking at each of us speculatively.

We responded like a Greek chorus.

"Go on, for heaven's sake."

"Well," she said, "to tell this part makes me a little fidgety.

"The men got out, took off their shoes and socks, rolled up their pants and pushed. Nothing happened. Then they tore out parts of hedges that marked off the fields and wedged them as much as they could under the back wheels. Lloyd didn't get the stickers out of his arms and legs for days.

"Claire Simon was the one who suggested we stop work, squeeze into our car and eat the lunch we'd brought. Everyone thought lunch was a good idea. We squeezed to make room for the men but we were all jammed together so tight the women were getting almost as wet from the men's clothes as the men already were. The two drivers were in the men's car ahead, the one that was stuck. We were munching our cheese and bread soddenly, not talking, when Claire made another suggestion. Lloyd was opening a bottle of wine. I remember every detail of what happened at this moment and afterwards. Claire laughed a little, but it was self-consciously, and she said:

" 'You remember last night on the boat, when we were having dinner and it was all so beautiful, Stephen proposed a libation to Poseidon as a kind of thank you and tribute for making his sea so beautiful and calm for us and we all thought that was a fine idea and everybody poured a little of his wine over the side of the boat?' Of course we remembered. 'Well, we didn't make any offering to Zeus, and the gods, you know, are supposed to be very jealous.'

"We got the idea at once and each of us handed his glass over to the ones on the outside, so a little wine was poured into the rain from every glass."

Ellen stopped again and we prodded her impatiently.

"Well." She was a little defiant. "You probably think this was all very silly but we were so wet and cold and discouraged we were glad of any distraction to take our minds off our own misery and the endless talk, while we were huddled in our car and the men were plowing back and forth with brambles, of how we were ever going to get out of this slough of despond. That's what Stephen had named it, you know, from *Pilgrim's Progress,* and he had said earlier if we ever did get out he was going to leave behind a marker of some kind like staking out the North Pole. Anyway this is what actually happened, and it couldn't have been more than a minute after the last libation had gone over the side of the car. There were two shattering claps of thunder, one immediately after the other, following two zigzags of lightning over the mountaintops ahead of us. Until that moment there had not been one sound of thunder nor even a distant flicker of lightning. I don't remember that anybody said a word, and I'm sure everyone knew as surely as I knew that something was going to happen, so we just sat staring and waiting. We didn't wait long, maybe two minutes.

"The two drivers in the car ahead began yelling, jumped out of the car waving their arms, jumping up and down, turning back to us and pointing ahead, and we saw two tractors coming. Their drivers blew their horns to let us know they saw and heard us and turned in our direction. They couldn't have been nicer or more friendly and efficient. They hitched our cars to theirs, took us down the mountain they had just climbed, and there was Sparta.

"One thing I forgot to say," Ellen added. "Lloyd was the first one out of our car. When he stood on the ground he stopped, looked around and put out his hand with the palm up the way you do, and as he started toward the drivers of the tractor he called to us, 'The rain has stopped.' "

There was nothing supernatural about the birth of my twins but the circumstances around it were as improbable as those around Ellen's story, though the connection between the two is of the utmost remoteness. At some time during that evening around the fire Sophy urged me to tell it, and the fact that Ellen had dared our incredulity gave me the courage to challenge theirs. I cannot remember a time when I was not fascinated by personal incidents of the unlikely coincidence. I realize this almost morbid interest is because for years I have been chafed by accusations, about anything I have told, of overstatement. When my twins happened to be born on Labor Day, I had a telegram from a dear friend that read, "You always did exaggerate." Once more I affirm I do not exaggerate one detail of the happenings of their birth on September 2, in a year of grace.

Some weeks before that date my obstetrician had told me this was to be a Caesarean birth, and included several instructions, severely and emphatically given, that at the first faint indication of labor I was to notify him at once and come immediately to the hospital. This was some forty minutes' drive into town from the suburb of Philadelphia in which we lived. A friend of more years and means than ours, learning this requirement and urgency, insisted that simultaneously with the call to the obstetrician she must be informed; she would have her car and chauffeur on call for that moment. They would reach me far more quickly than John, my husband, could come from his job at the far side of the city.

About a week before this plan was put into operation, a friend of John's telephoned he was in America. Like John he was British and they had been at Cambridge together. John immediately asked him to stay with us. When I was told this I asked who the friend was.

"Old Bunjie, one of the best. You'll like him, I'm sure, though I doubt he's ever met an American."

This left in the air what response I might kindle in Bunjie at any time, but particularly when I would not be putting my best foot forward; even more specifically in the present circumstances, my foot could scarcely be seen at all.

Bunjie arrived, a silent but pleasant man. I remember his tweed jackets with pockets that always sagged from the tobacco and pipes he carried in them. I have no recollection of his face; most of it was hidden a great deal of the time by his pipe. In the daytime he walked, taking with him our two dogs, a Great Dane and a Sealyham. The Great Dane was named Multash and I do not know from what source John had derived it. The Sealyham, I explained to Bunjie, was named Cherry because our colored cook had said the first time she saw him he made her think of "Swing Low, Sweet Chariot." When I told him this there was a silence while Bunjie, ruminating, filled his pipe. When it was lighted and giving him satisfaction, he inquired:

"Now tell me, how did you happen to think of the name Cherry? Odd name for a dog, what?" He did not inquire about the origin of Multash. This must have seemed to him sensible and appropriate.

In the evenings the two men reminisced happily about Brains, Rolly, Toodle and other friends, whose exploits and pithy sayings in my unvoiced opinion were not sensational. I knitted tiny garments until the evening ended for them with a small whiskey—I never heard John say Scotch because for him there was only one whiskey—a splash of soda, certainly no ice, then we went up to bed.

One morning about a week after Bunjie's arrival I felt a twinge. Only the doctor's emphasis made me take notice of it. However, I opened the program set down for me with a telephone call to the doctor and another to Nancy, for the car and James. I caught Bunjie as he was starting his morning walk with the dogs, called him back to the house, and apologizing for delaying him, gave the telephone numbers of the hospital and John's office. Would he notify the hospital that I was on my way and tell John to meet me there? I had a few last-minute things to put into my bag and must check once more with the household the routine to be followed in my absence.

When I came out to the car I was astonished to find Bunjie waiting there. I remonstrated that this was not included in the entertainment of a guest even in America. He told me to get into the car and stop nattering, he was not going to let old John down. After telling me John had been out of the office when he had called but the message had been left to meet us at the hospital, my companion put his pipe in his mouth, though he did not light it, and there was no more conversation the rest of the way into town. I had a number of things to think about but I would have welcomed a distraction from them.

John, arriving at his office, had felt a disquietude that would not let him settle down to work. He thought, he told me later, of telephoning back to the house to make sure I was all right but had not wanted to communicate any apprehension. He decided instead to come home, making up on the way some excuse for his return—like paper work that needed solitude —something that would justify his staying close by. The instant he had made this decision, he explained later, and resentfully, instead of feeling reassured he had felt even more unhappy, so that by the time he had got out the car and started for home he was jumpy with nerves. As he put it, "quite irrational."

Total dementia is in my opinion an inadequate diagnosis of his reaction to the sight of Bunjie and me coming toward him in a strange car. He thought we were eloping. The likelihood of a man running away with a woman who momentarily expected a baby and looked it is difficult to conjecture, but to John at the moment, this was the only possible explanation of our being on the road.

By the time he'd become a rational man again, reason, prevailing at last, telling him Bunjie and I were on the way to the hospital, the realization so flooded him with increased anxiety he first stalled the car and then very nearly stripped the gears. Endeavoring to turn around, he backed into another car. By the time he had exchanged imprecations and insurance cards with the other driver and finally gotten under way again, we were long out of sight.

A nurse was waiting just inside the door when Bunjie and I reached the hospital. My doctor had told her, she explained, to take us straight to my room; we need not stop at the desk to fill in the forms that are required and take considerable time. Bunjie, realizing he was being included, shied visibly and tried to bolt.

"Oh, no, Mr. Wrench." The nurse patted his arm. "You don't have to leave her yet. She'll want to have you around, I know, until she has to leave."

My intention was to explain the situation and release Bunjie but a full-bodied pain caught me and I clamped my jaws together.

"Bring her suitcase and take her other arm, Mr. Wrench," the nurse ordered. "We've got to keep going."

Bunjie was in shock, apparently. His mouth was open but there was no sound from him, though I could hear him beside me breathing noisily.

Another nurse and a doctor were waiting in the room I was to occupy. At the doorway Bunjie dropped my suitcase, wheeling around for a takeoff, but our usherette caught him with an iron grip on his arm.

"I'll take you to the room where fathers wait." She led him off, his mouth still open.

Very shortly my activities were curtailed by anesthesia. What happened to the bystander, Bunjie, the most innocent of them all, I learned from John some days later.

John had arrived at the hospital wild-eyed, he admitted, and demanding at the desk my whereabouts, was told he was not permitted above the first floor; only an immediate relative was allowed to accompany the patient. John's bellowed announcement of his relationship was received with frowning disapproval as an attempt at jocularity thoroughly out of place. The more John protested that the man who had gone upstairs with me was an impostor, not intentionally, actually a friend who happened to be staying at the house, the more violently inarticulate he became. His incoherence was aggravated by the icy disbelief of the receptionist. When he pounded on the desk, she spoke and he heard her. It was the voice of authority to a child who was having a tantrum. He would either take a seat in the general waiting room downstairs or he must leave the hospital. John felt no doubt, he said, that she would see either program enforced. Momentarily silenced, he was wildly formulating some other plan —perhaps a telephone call from a booth outside that would bypass her for a sympathetic ear—when my father walked into the hospital and joined him at the desk.

My father had given us no word of his intention to come on from Chicago for the accouchement, but knowing it was imminent and egged on by my stepmother, had taken the train the night before, telephoned the house from the station, learned my whereabouts and come straight there. Without difficulty he established his own identity and, not so easily, John's. A nurse's aide was summoned to bring them to my room but when they reached it I had already been wheeled away. The sight of the empty room brought John to the very brink of total collapse. My father had to take his arm to steer him in the wake of the nurse's aide. There was only one occupant of the waiting room for parents when they reached it, unhappy Bunjie. He and John wrung hands silently. Father surmised the two men knew each other but no introduction was made to him. He said the stranger opened his mouth to let a few guttural sounds escape and John answered them with:

"I know, I know, old fellow. Just stand by, won't you?"

Bunjie obeyed this request literally but Father sat down on a chair by a table, took from it a magazine and endeavored to read. There was no further talk, unless the guttural sounds from the unknown were interpreted as speech.

Father did not remember how long they waited; several days, he thought, admitting this was unlikely. At a noise of furniture moving he looked up from his magazine to see John not merely pacing, but pacing off the room with industry and concentration. He was taking in his stride its dimensions.

As Father watched with interest, John took from his inner pocket a notebook and pencil and wrote down the estimated length, width of the room and the diagonal distance from corner to corner. To be fair and accurate, he had moved toward the center the furniture that had prevented his start with heel to one baseboard and ending with toe pressing the opposite one.

A nurse interruped his work. Father did not know she was the one who had brought Bunjie and me to my room. He saw she carried a small medicine glass and smelled ammonia as she passed him on her way straight to Bunjie. Reaching him, without a word she pushed him down into a chair in front of which he happened to be standing. With one hand she seized his forelock and tilted back his head, with the other poured ammonia into his mouth, which he opened involuntarily, unless, as Father said, it might have been open all the time.

"Mr. Wrench," she said, "you have beautiful twin daughters and Mrs. Wrench is just fine." When I interrupted at this point Father's account of the story: "Didn't you explain to the nurse? Where was John?" Father defended himself.

"I was astonished at the news of twins and thankful you were all right—and John wasn't there. I just stood staring at that man trying to get his breath and the nurse grabbing his head—it could have been attached to a rubber hose from the look of it. Then the nurse shook my hand but, thank God, she'd used up all the ammonia she'd brought and she left the room. Because I was dazed, I suppose, because I thought it was so important to straighten out the paternity, I called after her, 'You made a mistake about—'

"She wheeled round and stood in the doorway.

" 'Oh, no I haven't. It's twins, and they're beautiful.' She was gone.

" 'Why in the name of God didn't *you* tell her?' I said to John, and he wasn't there. I said, 'Where's John?' but I might as well have been talking to myself. That man I was with in prime condition was no talker, and now all he did was wave a flabby hand in a kind of circular motion and shake his head, whatever that meant. I didn't know how John could have got out of that room. He had certainly been in it when the nurse arrived, and it was not a room you could get lost in. I felt a need to sit down and went over to the couch. It was well away from the wall, where John had pulled it to get to the baseboard for his measuring. Automatically I tried to push it back into place but I could scarcely move it an inch. I looked over the back to see what it had caught on. It was John stretched full length, just coming to. He had been in the act of measuring when the nurse had come in, and hearing the news had fainted quietly on the spot."

Some days later I asked John about Bunjie. I'd had flowers from him. John said when he and Father had got home that night of the double-header day, Bunjie was gone. The report of the household was that he'd come in a taxi, kept it waiting, gone up and packed his bag and left. Two or three weeks later John showed me a letter thanking us for our hospitality and saying he'd gone straight back to England. He was going to raise Sealyhams. I wonder what he named them. Come to think of it, I never knew Bunjie's name either.

VI

Family Codes

One day recently at a cocktail party I was talking to a friend who is a particular joy to see not only for herself but because she is so well tailored; hairline, hemline never drooping. We saw at the same moment her husband come in with a small group of late arrivals and she waved to him. When he had joined us she said:

"Emily, please forgive us, I'll explain another time, but, Harry, my shoes are worn out."

"O.K.," was her husband's answer, "let's go." They made their way to the door.

She telephoned the next day to ask if I would lunch with her. Across our eggs Benedict she apologized for their abrupt departure the day before. I interrupted.

"I knew something had happened that made you want to get away quickly, but I recognize a family code when I hear it. What was the message, if it isn't a secret?"

Kay admitted it was a code but not secret. Then she told me.

"Years ago when my cousin Fred was a little boy he went

to spend the night with a friend. It was the first night he'd ever been away from home.

"All afternoon they played together, having a good time, but when it got dark Fred suddenly realized he didn't want to spend the night. He went in the house to the little boy's mother, and told her he was very sorry but he had to go home immediately. The poor woman was evidently surprised by this unexpectedness and I'm sure very inconvenienced about getting the child back. She asked him why he thought he must go. Evidently it hadn't occurred to Fred he would have to explain this sudden decision, but he met the crisis.

" 'Because,' he said, 'my shoes are worn out.' Certainly she took him home.

"The little boy's mother told Fred's, and his irrefutable explanation became family vocabulary. When you heard me use it at the cocktail party I had just seen another man coming in at the same time as Harry. That man invariably tries to bait me and make snide jokes about my 'causes.' He always says the word in capital letters. I just didn't feel up to coping with him so I told Harry."

If I were offered a wager that somewhere there exists a family that does not use among its members a word or phrase of special meaning I would accept that wager on the spot and double the bet. I declare categorically and challenge denial that wherever there is a group closely associated, incidents are shared, and remembered. Gradually, reference to any of them becomes abbreviated and applied to other situations. Given time, these references become a code intimately understood. I repeat, for insistence, every family has one.

Sometimes when a piece of family lore is shared with an outsider it is prefaced by a credit line: "My grandmother used to say," or "An uncle of mine . . ." I like very much an opinion originally voiced by Anne Page, John's Great-Aunt Mary.

"When the good Lord calls me," she had said, "I hope to be ready but I'm in no hurry." Anne says her children and her grandchildren use part of it for something unhappily anticipated: "I'm in no hurry."

My granddaughter Eliza was riding in a horse show this fall when her wretched pony relieved itself spectacularly in the ring. Another grandchild, Alis, sitting beside me, exploded into one squeal of laughter and immediately clapped a hand over her mouth. Though her eyes brimmed with tears of joy, I heard her mutter fiercely to herself a phrase I recognized. Startled, I said evidently she knew that story, and she nodded. "Mommie told me." "Mommie" and her twin sister had been four years old when they created this story; now it had become family language.

We lived outside Philadelphia and on Sunday afternoons, as a family we went to the house of friends a few miles away. Their house was on a considerable acreage and to take advantage of this they had instituted one of the happiest programs I have ever known. In the spring and the fall their friends were asked to come every Sunday afternoon with their children for outdoor games in a meadow. All ages were accommodated to the games or the games to them. Parents, even grandparents puffed up and down the field; when they dropped out from want of breath, they joined other panting rooters on the sidelines.

A lofty teen-ager would share his base with a six-year-old. Only the smallest fry were fenced in a separate play yard supervised by the family nanny. When parents threatened to lie down on the field, the games were called off. Then the

group separated, the teen-agers to a playroom for more noise and for refreshments, the old weaklings to the library for tea or stronger, the little ones to the nursery for milk and cookies.

To my twins these Sunday afternoons were weekly excursions to paradise, the days between of interminable dullness. Shortly after their initiation into this happy throng, however, they entered an exasperating behavior phase. I have no idea what began it. Anna, their nurse, and I were without prudery; but suddenly one day anything connected with the bathroom became a reason for giggling. The word "bathroom" whispered between them would induce paroxysms of joyful hoots; anything associated with that room from fixtures to functions was even funnier. I was bewildered, dismayed and mortified by this sudden display of lewdness. Reluctantly, and only because I had reached a point of desperation, I confided to two friends of longer and wider parental experience than mine this depravity my little cherubs were enjoying. To my astonishment each assured me this was a phase common to all children, and each gave the same advice.

"Ignore it," one said. "Make the act a flop," said the other. "It's just a bid for attention. They want an audience and if they don't get it they'll try something else."

Following my principle—either do what the doctor tells you or don't bother to go to a doctor—I told Anna we would both follow the prescription offered. We followed. We ignored, ignored, ignored. Nothing changed; still the giggling and the unrestrained happy laughter.

One day I knew I had reached the bottom of the bottle and could not take another dose. I made up my own prescription. I took them into my bedroom, closed the door, set them side by side on a couch and myself on a chair in front and I talked to them. I told them Anna and I had noticed they

97

liked to laugh about bathroom things. (To say we had noticed was a Mount Everest of understatement.) This was of no interest to us—the hell it wasn't, was my inner thought—but it did show what babies they were. I had thought they were growing up to be people, but I must have been mistaken because they were still little babies. Grownups didn't think those things were funny because everybody had a potty just the way everybody had a bed or a chair and that wasn't funny. I had their attention; I felt I had reached the moment for a crafty suggestion, seasoned with a little bribery. I was not lowering my standards in this. I had practiced consistently, according to circumstances, either the application of the palm of my hand to the buttocks of the offenders, or a tempting bit of cajolery. The manual technique in this instance seemed to me thoroughly inappropriate. I was ready for the other and prayed they were. I reminded them of the Sunday afternoons at the Geyelins'; but—I think I paused dramatically at that —babies were not allowed.

"Now," I said, "I'm afraid I'm going to have to telephone Mrs. Geyelin you aren't so grown up as she thought; you are still babies."

They were people, they assured me. Very grown-up big people. They had stopped being babies that very minute. They would never laugh again at the silly things babies laugh at. Never. They would show me.

The warning in those words passed me by; I was exulting in my handling of the situation with an inward *yah, yah* to my experienced friends and advisers.

The following Sunday afternoon we went to the Geyelins'. When the games were finished and the groups separated, fresh arrivals from the neighboring countryside came in for tea. One of these said to me:

"I hear your twins are here. I'm dying to see them." Turning to the hostess, "Couldn't they come down for just a minute?" Over my protests she agreed politely, and sent word for the children to come downstairs.

They stood in the doorway holding hands, pink-cheeked, wide-eyed. I called in the idiot voice only mothers use:

"Come in, darlings, and say how do you do." They went round the circle of some twenty people and each one of them as she shook hands said gravely, to the speechless astonishment of the recipient:

"How do you do. Everybody has a potty, everybody has a toilut"—Anna's deplorable word—"and it is *not* funny."

At the horse show, Alis, my granddaughter, had checked her laughter with "Everybody has a potty. It's *not* funny."

When one of my daughters says, "Why, Bishop Wright," she knows the source of that phrase. I am not sure my grandchildren do but they all use it to another member of the family as a terse, derisive comment on some addlepated banality another member has uttered. We owe the origin of the phrase to my grandmother and the happy chance that my grandfather overheard her use it. In Indianapolis, my grandmother followed one of the social customs of those days, an "at home." During the season of these events, particular days were specified on the invitations that went out in the early fall. These "at homes" were tea parties, though I have been told hot chocolate, bountifully topped with whipped cream, was the preferred refreshment. My grandmother received her guests at a wide entrance arch to the parlor, and frequently Grandfather Wiles joined her because, he pointed out, gentlemen often dropped in to these "affairs." Grandmother's wry comment was that he enjoyed the company of ladies and paid no attention to the gentlemen.

Since her particular enjoyment was in the company of gentlemen, this was an arrangement agreeable to both.

One Monday, or whatever day of the week was allotted to these titillating occasions, Grandmother was in her bedroom completing her toilette when a maid brought her the distressing news Bishop Wright had arrived and was waiting in the parlor. Shocked by the impropriety of her tardiness and understandably flustered, she hurried from her room to the stairs. This was a steep flight terminating in a broad entrance hall, polka-dotted with small Oriental carpets known as prayer rugs or scatter rugs. Beneath them the floor was waxed to duplicate the surface of an ice skating rink. Grandfather Wiles said they were called scatter rugs because that was the way you were likely to find bones and brains of people walking on them. In her agitated rush Grandmother, a dignified but always an impulsive woman, who seldom moved slowly, tripped on the top step. Had she gone headfirst she might well have justified Grandfather's description of the rugs as a depository, but she landed instead sitting down and in this position descended the flight buckety-buckety and, ending up at the bottom on one of the rugs, rode on this carpet across the hall into the parlor and to the feet of the Bishop. At the sound of this staccato descent that gentleman had risen to his feet and watched, with what emotion I can only guess, his hostess' approach. As he bent down, assisting her to stand —and Grandfather, coming in the front door at that moment, joyfully heard her—she said:

"Why, Bishop Wright, I never come downstairs that way."

Savoring this in repetition, Grandfather maintained it was a pity to create and shatter simultaneously a picture of Grandmother habitually using this form of rapid progress.

One night my father, my stepmother, Achsah, my daughter

B and I were playing a card game called, I think, Oklahoma. I have not played it since and I have no recollection of how it was played then, but that evening we had been taught the game. The only thing I do remember is the phrase it brought into family use. My stepmother was wearing a delectable robe, called then a tea gown, of pale green velvet with a cascade of lace down the front and a train. At a point in the game when evidently my father thought he was about to make a coup, my stepmother outmaneuvered him. He put down his remaining cards, looked across the table at her with affectionate but rueful exasperation and suggested:

"Why don't you go down to the firehouse, dear, and talk to the boys?"

B and Achsah looked at each other in bewilderment at the suggestion, and at my joyous laughter. Neither of them had lived in a small town. They could not savor the full flavor of my father's proposal. In Muncie, Indiana, where my father was born and I was too, the men in the fire department, when not in action on pleasant days, sat on straight chairs tilted back against the front of the firehouse on Main Street. They watched the world go by. No lady would ever have dreamed of stopping to talk to them but there was little that escaped their notice and comments. Therefore, a waggish comment on a particularly fruity tidbit of gossip was invariably, "You must have got that from the boys at the firehouse."

When her children are provoking her, B says, "Why don't you go down to the firehouse?" It is a signal to clear out and they obey it.

Achsah has brought into the family, by way of a bishop other than my grandmother's, a phrase we have all adopted. Its source, and it may be apocryphal, is a story of a benign, kindly gentleman, a Bishop Anderson, who lived in Saint

Paul, where Achsah's family has its roots. Walking along a residential street one wintry day, the saintly man saw a little boy on the porch of a house he was passing. The little boy, too short to reach it, was trying to press the doorbell by jumps that were ineffectual. He had taken off his mittens in order to reach the bell more accurately but was having to stop intermittently to blow on his hands. The Bishop promptly changed his direction, went up the steps onto the porch and, one arm protectively around the boy's shoulders, with his free hand pushed the bell vigorously. This done, he smiled down at the poor little waif shut out, because he was so small and helpless, from the warmth of home.

The little waif, looking up at him, said:

"Now we run like hell." As he followed his own counsel, the front door was opened to the Bishop. Somewhat distorted, it has become a family slogan of advice in a touchy situation: "Run like Bishop Anderson."

When a friend, trying to assemble from the directions I was reading aloud to her a kitchen device she had ordered, muttered, red-faced with fury, "Yah—the men will know," I knew this was family language. After her anger had been diminished by putting all the pieces back in the box and the box in the trashcan, I had the temerity to ask the source of "the men's" knowledge. She managed to laugh a little and told me. Her husband, whom I knew as a distinguished writer, had a mechanical knowledge, she said, barely sufficient for the replacing of a burned-out electric light bulb. Among their friends another couple lived under the same imbalance. The husband, a scholar and recognized authority in his field, had never been able to remember, for instance, which way to turn a valve to bring heat into a radiator or shut it off. The two men one summer had decided to buy together a small boat with outboard motor in which to take their sons fishing. It seemed expedient to the two wives to accompany their husbands when the purchase was made. The salesman, a dapper young man of massive self-assurance and amiability, had devoted his attention exclusively to the two husbands. Each wife, recognizing on her husband's face a well-known expression of vacant incomprehension, had ventured to interrupt the young man's torrential salesmanship with a few pertinent questions about operation and repair. The orator had not paid the slightest attention. Finally annoyed, my friend had asked sharply for an answer to her question and the young man with pitying condescension had answered:

"Dear lady, the *men* will know."

Their unspoken reply, mouthed to each other, was "*What* men?"

Mother's family was of the Society of Friends, and although after her marriage she went to the Presbyterian church with Father, she always used Quaker speech to her relatives and other Friends and maintained some Quaker customs. One of these was silent grace at meals. A cousin on Mother's side of the family, Alida Marsh, came to spend the night with us when she was about five years old and I was the same age. Alida was one of five children. Mother said afterward, probably by the time she came along her parents had stopped explaining why they did certain things, and she had simply fallen unquestioningly into the pattern. My memory of the evening she was with us is only that we had supper with my mother and father. That was unusual, but certainly I know the incident because it was transplanted into family language. Evidently Alida had felt uneasy as a visitor but lifting her head after silent grace, with a deep sigh of contentment she had said:

"This is just like home. We smell our plates too."

I knew Alida's words had come into family language when, some thirty years later, I heard my daughter A consoling B, B wishing aloud she'd never accepted an invitation to a weekend house party; she had never been there before, she probably wouldn't know anybody.

"You'll have a good time; you won't feel strange. They probably smell their plates too," A told her.

When a group of friends shares an experience, a phrase from it sometimes becomes a coin of their realm and it is used from then on among them. In 1956 or thereabouts, five good companions, and I was one of them, traveled canals in England and Wales on a boat we chartered. Howard Lindsay and his wife, Dorothy Stickney, were members of our nautical party. Howard plunged with such enthusiasm into the life of water men, he bought and wore a yachting cap, and one day with a man-of-the-sea nonchalance told the captain he believed he would take a turn at running the boat. Hearing this and the captain's acquiescence, the rest of us moved involuntarily into his immediate vicinity, not to be back-seat drivers, only to watch with interest—and some apprehension. We all saw a boat bearing down on us from the right—we thought it affected of us to say starboard—but Sophy, the only genuine sailor, knew, as she explained later, a fundamental rule afloat: the vessel on your starboard has the right of way. The knowledge broke her silence.

"Howard"—her voice was sharp with authority—"there's a boat to starboard."

Howard nodded complacently. "*He* sees me," he said.

There was no collision, only a few angry words from the skipper as his craft swerved from ours. Dorothy explained later:

"That's the way Howard drives a car. When I tell him we're going to be hit, he always says, '*He* sees me.' It's hard on the nerves—mine—but," she added ruminatively, "we never have been hit."

Since that day, any one of us, wishing to shrug away personal responsibility, is likely to say, "*He* sees me."

Each one of us, too, in that happy band has appropriated another phrase from the Lindsays. Howard said its origin was an old vaudeville joke. An actor stranded in a small town was eating dinner in its one hotel. The waiter asked him:

"How is your soup, sir?"

The actor told him:

"I'm sorry I stirred it."

Of a situation in which unintentionally I have found myself involved, and deeply regret it, I say, with thanks to the Lindsays:

"I'm sorry I stirred it."

Lacking code phrases, communication within the family is without flavor is my assertion, and to share, outside the family, a code phrase is a stronger bond of friendship than a fraternity grip. To hear a family code used by a stranger, however, is a Popocatepetl of surprise. The code I heard at Bergdorf Goodman's in New York was not a phrase; it was a language.

When I was a child in Muncie, Indiana, Betty Ball was my closest friend. Our parents were friends and sometimes when they talked within our hearing about things they did not wish to share with us, they used a language that was, to our fury, incomprehensible. Suddenly, gleefully, we discovered the key. We never by look or smile let them know we had found a Rosetta stone—that was a pledge between us—and it was a long time before we admitted to each other what we were now able to translate was boring. Our own use of the language was more exciting. Well out of our parents' hearing we baffled and infuriated our contemporaries.

As in "The Hunting of the Snark," I skip forty years.

Something happened recently so astonishing I still doubt its credibility. I must reassure myself it did occur. Otherwise, I would never have broken our pledge of secrecy, and I hope Betty will forgive me. The key to the language is this: You must insert the letter *g* in every syllable of each word—a hard *g*. For example, "you must do this if the word has only one syllable" becomes: y-g-ou m-g-ust d-g-o th-g-is i-g-if th-g-e w-g-ord h-g-as, and so on.

One day a few weeks ago, I went into Bergdorf Goodman's late in the afternoon, so near to closing time I was the only customer in the department. Three or four of the salespeople were sitting together facing the stockroom, evidently waiting to make a quick departure when the closing bell rang. As I passed the group, one of the women, making no effort to lower her voice, spoke to her friends.

"I-g-i th-g-ink th-g-at i-g-is a-g-an a-g-actre-g-ess b-g-ut I-g-i d-g-on't kn-g-ow wh-g-o sh-g-e i-g-is."

A man with a gun directly pointed could not have stopped me more decisively. The years rolled back as fast as a movie film rewound. I was in Muncie again talking to Betty and the words came as trippingly from my tongue as if I really were.

"No, I am not an actress," I said in the language, "but I thank you very much."

The saleswoman who had spoken, screamed, jumped to her feet, clapped her hand over her mouth and bolted into the stockroom. Her friends, wide-eyed with apprehension, moved involuntarily more closely together. A woman coming from the stockroom intercepted me as I reached it.

"I'm extremely sorry, madam," she told me, "for any discourtesy. I'm sure it was not intentional. Miss Crandall"—I think that was the name—"is very upset."

The loyal friends, breaking their huddle, surrounded us, protesting, explaining no harm was meant, and I, trying to talk above them, said over and over what a happy moment this had been for me and could I please say so to Miss Crandall.

When Miss Crandall was finally persuaded to come back and, reassured, to talk to me, I learned this had been a language her parents and the parents of her best friend had used. She and her friend had one day discovered the secret of it and from then on had made it their own. Over the years she had forgotten about it until late one afternoon like today, she said, waiting to go home, and only one or two customers there, she had taught the language to her group. After that they had fun making comments about people around them "because," close to tears, she added, "I promised them there wasn't another living soul that understood the language. My parents and even my friend are dead and I never dreamed there was anybody else in the world who knew it." That, I told her, was just what I had thought.

So you see, Betty, it is not really our secret any more. That's why I have taught it to my grandchildren.

VII

Midsummer Nights

2090 Horatio Road
Cleveland, Ohio
March 15, 1971

Dear Miss Kimbrough:

Miss Dorothy Stickney suggested that I write you because she thought you would have information that would be of use on a study of Miss Margaret Anglin.

I have spent a year doing research on the career of Margaret Anglin in preparation for a doctoral dissertation at Chase Western Research University in Cleveland, Ohio. My dissertation will center on Miss Anglin's Greek productions which she produced between 1910 and 1930. . . . According to the program of the 1915 production you were in the chorus of *Medea* and also *Electra*. I thought you might perhaps feel like sending me some comments or thoughts on your experiences with Miss Anglin. . . .

I thank you for whatever help you may be able to give.

Sincerely,

Arnold Johnson

P.S. Miss Stickney did not know anything about Howard Lindsay's contribution to the 1915 production. Would you be able to tell me exactly what he did in the production? He is listed in the program as the assistant director.

Miss Stickney would not know anything about Howard Lindsay's contribution, I wrote in my answer to Mr. Johnson, because she was not married to him then; she had not met him in 1915. I met him then and I could tell Mr. Johnson more details of that summer than of last summer or the one before because the summer of 1915 was what I would have called the most thrilling time in my life. Thinking about it today, when my evaluations are more moderately voiced, I will not modify that description. I was fifteen years old that summer and I was on the stage in the company of Margaret Anglin. Mercifully for Mr. Johnson and his dissertation, I have not included in my letter to him the circumstances of my being there and, to him, other irrelevant details but in my own chronicle almost every detail is relevant to the miracle of the whole and this is how it began:

A cousin of my mother's, Dr. Richard Boone—I called him cousin Richard too—was a professor of philosophy at the University of California at Berkeley. He wrote Mother and her half sister Louisa—Aunt Lulie to me—urging them to come out for the summer to see the San Francisco Exposition; another professor, a friend, was going abroad with his family for the summer and his house would be available for us to rent. Aunt Lulie, a widow, and her son Charles—their last name was Robbins—lived in New York, where she taught at Columbia; we lived in Chicago.

There evidently was a spate of agitated correspondence between the sisters when this invitation came. I remember my father at breakfast suggesting there might be less confusion if one waited for an answer before writing a follow-up letter to the one preceding. I do not know that Mother followed this suggestion; I do know we went to California. Daddy went with us, stayed a week, and came back for our last week there.

We traveled both ways on the Santa Fe, train No. 3, the California Limited. We left Chicago at 8 P.M. the first Sunday in June and arrived in Oakland at 8:10 A.M. on Thursday.

The California Limited, its souvenir pamphlet said, "runs on rock-ballasted and oil-sprinkled tracks, safeguarded by block signals . . . equipped with compartment and compartment–drawing room sleepers . . . the entire train is ventilated by the Garland process. It is electric lighted throughout . . . electric fans are also provided."

I shared a compartment with my brother Charles, who was nine. Mother and Daddy had the adjoining one and there was a door between which could be opened. Brother and I had grimy hands and faces most of the time because we liked to sit facing each other, each one at a window so that we could look out, and we liked the windows open. Screens kept out rocks and pebbles the speed of the train kicked up, but let in dust, soot and small cinders. I always sat in the seat facing forward because riding backward made me carsick, overriding Brother's protest of this arrangement by telling him in great detail what would happen if we changed places. This was the reason he said he preferred to sit in the observation car at the end of the train. I know the reason was that he liked meeting and talking to people and I told him so, because everybody on the observation platform rode backward. When I was sent to bring him to bed one night I heard him say to his neighbor:

"I see that you have a great many more stars out here than we have at home."

When I told Mother I could not make him believe this wasn't true, she said she was only thankful to hear he had been talking about the stars. Each time she had gone to fetch him she had heard him sharing with all the occupants of the observation car minute details of our family life.

Hilda and Gertrude were in the car next to ours and Hilda was supposed to look after Brother. She did come in once in a while to scrub him down. She was our cook; Gertrude was her friend and had asked to come too in order to see the San Francisco fair. At Berkeley she shared a room with Hilda and was our waitress. When we got home to Chicago she went back to her other place, and we only saw her when she came to visit Hilda in our kitchen. At our house they were very quiet but on the train there happened to be a number of other Swedish people, with whom they made friends and had a gay time. They had all brought baskets of food; when I could not find Brother on the observation platform I knew he was in their car getting things to eat.

The day we arrived in Oakland Brother was not allowed to visit either of his favorite places. After he was washed he put on a blue linen suit of short pants and a sailor blouse with white braid around the collar. I remember hearing Mother tell Hilda, who had left her friends to come in and help us pack:

"I brought six suits and that's the last clean one."

He and I sat facing each other by the window but the windows were closed to keep us clean. It was so hot, sweat was trickling down our backs. My hair was long, pinned at the neck by a large barrette. The barrette marked the boundary I had reached after a stormy spring's battle for permission to put my hair "up." At least it wasn't hanging loose like a ten-year-old's but I told Brother bitterly if I had been allowed to put it up I wouldn't be so hot. He wasn't listening; he was an inventive boy. As I was complaining about my hair, holding its thick tail in the air away from my back, he slid off the seat facing me, went to the john in the corner, lifted its green velour lid, knelt down and put his face into it, pushing with his hand the pedal that released the aperture at the bottom. When he was dredged up by an exasperated parent as we were pulling into the station, his face was blacker than it had been on the observation car; he explained he had just been getting some fresh air to cool off. Mother was still making him spit into her handkerchief and wiping his face in the vestibule when the train stopped, the porter opened the door, and we came down the steps to the platform.

The Boones were waiting for us—cousin Richard, his wife and their grown-up son, Richard, Jr. With them was Aunt Lulie, short, plump, trim, quick—she fitted her name Robbins —with her sixteen-year-old son, Charles, tall, thin, slow, laconic. I heard him ask Brother if his face was striped like that from a disease; Charles had a scientist's detached curiosity. Brother explained his air-cooling invention and Charles approved it. "Good idea," he said. I doubt that the others noticed Brother's face, there was so much talking going on among them and so much to do: Hilda, Gertrude and their bags collected with ours, enough redcaps gathered to take care of it all, trunk checks turned in at the baggage counter and arrangements made for delivery in Berkeley. Finally we were on the ferry, everyone pointing out things for us to look at, no one interested in our telling them we had seen from the train real oranges on trees, and palms. Brother was interested in the ferry ride across the bay, but I was lofty about the experience, explaining I had been on a boat, from Hoboken to New York.

The first sight of the house routed the indifference I was trying hard to assume as my pattern for the summer. I had seen roses before in gardens and on trellises but I had never walked through a gate, up a gravel path to an entire facade, except for the doorway, so overlaid with pink roses it was impossible to see what the house itself was made of.

Inside the house I was taken aback by the library. I had never before seen or heard of one on a second floor, and it seemed to me a not very respectable place for it. We did not have a library in our apartment in Chicago, only bookshelves in the living room and the bedrooms, but at my grandfather's and any other house I knew, a library was on the first floor, always dark, and you had to wash your hands first if you were going to look at any of the books there. This one went all the way across the front of the house, with shelves to the ceiling between windows, a little movable ladder in front of them. Standing in the doorway, blinking in the sunlight, I shaded my eyes to see the room better. There were comfortable chairs and a big long table down the center with books, magazines on it. You could even come here in your nightgown, though I had certainly never heard of doing such a thing.

The rest of the house suited my idea of what was proper. Charles Robbins and my brother Charles had to share a room but I had one of my own, and since that was the only important requirement I was not interested in arrangements for the others. Aunt Lulie and her Charles had been there nearly a week so they knew where everything was and Aunt Lulie was impatient to show Mother the garden. Hilda and Gertrude were unpacking and said I was in the way, so I went too. The garden was the third surprise. It was big but not neat, there was lawn in the center, very green. The beds all the way around it were too wide to jump across—Brother tried—with the flowers jumbled in colors and kinds. Along the back there were trees. Orange and lemon and a kind I learned was avocado, and that was the summer I learned to eat avocado except that we called it alligator pear. Years later I heard the word "avocado" without an idea of what it meant.

The details of our trip and our arrival at the house are sharp in my memory, but there is a blur over the sequence of days that immediately followed. The red-letter one was so dazzling it put all others into shadow, brightened only by such moments as on the day Charles with Brother went on a hike into the hills: they took their lunch with them and brought back a bagful of snakes they emptied into the garden. I remember vaguely Charles' indignant explanation of the opportunity for study given by the proximity and the number of these harmless specimens, but what illuminated that day for me was the sight of Hilda taking a bag of garbage through the garden. Her purpose was to empty it into a large bin in a fenced-in small area at the far end. She did not empty it there nor in any one place. She had happened to choose for this daily excursion a time almost immediately after the moment when Charles had emptied his sack and gone with Brother into the house to invite their mothers to come and see the wonderful trophies of their hunt. Hilda was the first to see them and by heaven-sent timing I happened to be standing at my bedroom window that looked on the garden. Hilda saw one snake, dropped a few orange peels and announced her discovery with a bellow powerful

enough to be an echo of a Viking ancestor sighting the coast of Ireland. It brought Gertrude on a gallop from the kitchen. Hilda was on the gallop too, heading back for the house. Their collision knocked each runner on her back and spilled considerably more of the garbage. Whatever the Swedish word is for snakes, Hilda was using it in a rising crescendo and pointing. By the time the family reached them the daughters of Vikings were up on their feet again, both yelling. I stayed at the window, of course; it was the best seat in or out of the house. Even from the second floor I counted six snakes. Hilda and Gertrude agreed there were two hundred. Charles stated categorically and sulkily there were twenty; that was as many as he had been able to find. I am sure Charles was right, but they scattered so widely, their number could have seemed greater. It was a joyous sight to watch but not one to talk about; the topic was forbidden. Mother and Aunt Lulie cooked our supper; Hilda and Gertrude were given the evening off. The rest of the summer Charles and Brother alternated emptying the garbage. The snakes went back to the hills, to Charles' disgust and Hilda's disbelief.

We went to the fair several times, I remember. It was beautiful. My legs ached and I had to go find Charles and Brother when it was time to go home. I remember too trying to impress my cousin Richard Boone because I had a crush on him and had been told he was a great scholar, so I took long walks every morning before breakfast in the direction I thought he would go. I carried *The Autocrat of the Breakfast Table* because of all the books in the rented house, this seemed to me the most intellectual. I sat down at a place I thought my cousin would pass and read the book, not much of it because I found it dull. My cousin did not once pass that way; I have not read it since.

If coming events do cast shadows before, the first of these was a tea party given by the Boones to which Mother and Aunt Lulie were invited, and I was not. This selection was agreeable to me. I had been included in one party that in my opinion turned out to be very flat. The guest of honor had been David Starr Jordan, and I was told he had been president of Leland Stanford University and was an ichthyologist. I recognized the Greek sound of this because I had been reading Greek from an early age, thanks to an idea of Mother's she wanted to try out. At the Girls' Classical School in Indianapolis, her alma mater, Greek and Latin had been part of the curriculum in the primary grades. Because of her delight in them, and wanting me to share it, she reasoned that since to a child all letters looked strange and were difficult to copy and remember, Greek would be no more baffling than English; so she taught me to read Greek before I went to school. At Miss Faulkner's School in Chicago I had continued Greek, but not brilliantly. When I heard the word "ichthyologist" I associated it with *ichor*, which I happened to know was the word for the blood of the gods, so I went to the party for David Starr Jordan with high hopes of stories with lots of blood in them. When I asked Dr. Jordan if he would tell some bloody stories he looked surprised. When I reminded him tartly I thought that was his specialty, he told me apologetically it was fish, and not much blood to be got out of them. Between my mortification and my disappointment, the party sank into interminable tedium. Possibly I showed my glum disapproval of it because I was not invited to another.

Came the day and the party. Mother was calling me as she came home, up the path to the house. We met on the stairs.

"Come into my room," she said, "while I take off my things. I've something to tell you."

Mother had an exasperating habit of drawing out any piece of good news; bad news she always told quickly and directly. She pulled off her white kid gloves, one finger at a time, blew into them and put them in her glove case on the dressing table. She took off her hat and put it carefully into a hatbox, talking half to herself.

"I don't think I have ever made such an idiotic, fatuous remark in my life and I devoutly pray I'll never make another one of such inanity. Now sit down, not on the bed." (This was never permitted.) "I'm sure you've heard Aunt Lulie and me talking about going to the plays in the Greek Theater this summer?" I nodded. "Well, you'll never guess for whom the Boones' party was given today. They hadn't put it on the invitation because they weren't sure she could come. It was Margaret Anglin."

Certainly I knew who Margaret Anglin was—no ichthyologist. Whenever my allowance permitted, I always bought a copy of *Theatre* magazine, cut out of it and kept in a scrapbook the photographs of actresses and actors I had seen, had a crush on or hoped to see. I had pictures of Margaret Anglin, though I had never seen her. I knew she was one of the greatest, and I could have recited her biography and a list of plays in which she had been a star.

"You didn't actually meet her?" Mother nodded, and visibly blushed.

"I was so taken aback, I told her I had been delighted to learn she was giving three Greek plays out here this summer because—my daughter was studying Greek and this would be such an incentive to her. As if this was why Margaret Anglin had come to California."

"Oh, Mother." I was blushing for her.

"I know, I know. Blithering idiocy but let's not dwell on it. Now this is what she said, that great woman: perhaps

since you were so interested in Greek"—Mother shuddered
—"you—would—like—to watch—the—rehearsals."

If, before fainting, the room you are in spins around and
you feel violently sick at your stomach, then I was close to
it. Mother must have sensed something like this might happen, because she had answered Miss Anglin, with far more
than her usual kind of remark, that if I recovered from the
swoon into which such an invitation would undoubtedly send
me, she was sure I would indeed like to watch the rehearsals.
"They begin tomorrow," she added.

Perhaps I slept that night; I doubt it. I was dressed and
ready to go at half past six. Mother came out of her room
as I was tiptoeing down the stairs.

"You will have to wait until eight o'clock—all right, all
right, half past seven then," as I had started to protest. And
looking at my face, added, "You needn't eat breakfast." She
knew I would lose it. One of the reasons I was trying to get
out of the house was my anxiety that Mother would go with
me, as if I were a little girl being taken to the first day of
school. My relief that this was not suggested was so great, I
accepted the later departure without protest. I have no recollection of how I filled that interminable hour.

The theater was within easy walking distance of our house.
I ran most of the way. My cousin Richard had taken me to
see it when he was showing us the university. There had
been no performance or rehearsal going on so he had sent us
to the top row and when we reached it had stood on the
stage and said, scarcely above a whisper, the "Friends, Ro-
mans, countrymen" speech. We had heard every word as
clearly as if we had stood beside him. That morning as I ran
up a hill and through a woods to reach it, I knew for the first
time the pungent smell of eucalyptus. In 1943, on the morn-

ing of my first day of work in Hollywood, I had breakfast on a little balcony outside my apartment. As I came on the balcony in the early morning, I took a deep breath and was on the instant running up a hill in Berkeley, California, in 1915, and knew simultaneously the reason for my flight in time. The trees fringing my balcony were eucalyptus. In 1955 I was climbing a hill to reach the great theater at Epidaurus. I stopped suddenly because I was on another hill running through eucalyptus trees and these at Epidaurus were eucalyptus.

When I came into it, the theater was as empty as it had been on the day of our sightseeing tour with cousin Richard. I learned later rehearsals began at ten. It was not quite eight o'clock when I stopped running and in order not to be noticed sidled through the nearer of the two wide entrances that flanked the bowl. They would be used by the audience and sometimes during the performances were entrances and exits for the players. On our sightseeing visit I had thought the theater big, like a football stadium, where I had once seen a game. A football stadium filled with people is a bandbox compared to my impression of the Greek Theater when I stood alone in it. I knew I had never seen so big a place so exposed. If I climbed to the top row where I had heard cousin Richard speak I would be as easily spotted as if I stood in the middle of the stage. I very nearly followed the course of the French king who marched up a hill and then marched down again, yet I said to myself as I climbed up the outside edge to a halfway bench, "I was invited to come," but I was not surprised to realize I was walking on tiptoe. When I stopped tiptoeing and actually sat down, I knew on the instant here I was at last and here I would stay. During the two hours I was alone, I was as exposed to the sun as to anyone who might come, and the sun was hot. I stuck to the seat with as much sweat as determination.

Then they were all there. I heard them less than a minute before they came through the entrance I had used. They made a large group, everyone talking, calling to one another. These were real actors and actresses and it surprised me a little that they were talking and laughing like ordinary people. One of them, nodding his head toward the other side of the theater, said something and they all stopped talking. A woman was coming down the opposite ramp, a man on either side of her. I had no idea who the two men were but I knew two things simultaneously: the woman was Margaret Anglin, and having your heart turn over could actually happen. I could not see Miss Anglin's face nor the color of her hair because she wore a white hat with a broad drooping brim. She said, "Good morning, good morning," laughed and added, "Like every other one here, it's a lovely day." That was my true and lasting recognition of Miss Anglin. I would not need to see her features nor the color of her hair. I have never heard a voice so rich and full, though soft, with a curious little break, like a grace note in it; and this was not the rapture of a fifteen-year-old. To this day I have not heard a voice of that special quality. I am sure of this because the sound of it is as recognizable in my ear today as the tune of "The Star-Spangled Banner."

The two groups met at the foot of the ramp below the center of the stage. There was some discussion between them I could not hear. Then they scattered. Some moved up the steps onto the stage, others sat down along the front- and second-row benches. Perhaps there were thirty or forty people all told; I did not count. Miss Anglin sat down in the center of the front row, the same men who had come with her on either side. She spread open on her lap a large book in a black cover. The script of the play, I suppose, though I did not know then the word "script."

"Does anyone know if Mr. Platt is here?" As she spoke she looked around the theater and unmistakably caught sight of me. I saw her turn to the men on either side of her and nod in my direction. They looked where she indicated and like any crowd following something noticed by one or two people, so did most of the company turn my way. I was leaning forward, half standing in my excitement to get a better view of them. At that moment I wished I was flat on the ground, underneath the bench. I knew what I must do, but I was not sure my knees were steady enough to carry me. I reached Miss Anglin by saying to myself I *had* to do it. When I spoke, my own mother would not have recognized my wavering treble.

"I am Emily Kimbrough," I said. "Mother met you yesterday and you told her I might watch rehearsals."

Miss Anglin smiled immediately and put out her hand. She was a woman of iron control, because she did not wince when I put my hand in hers and it must have been like taking from a bed a hot water bottle that had been put there the night before.

"Of course," she said, and to the two men, "Emily is studying Greek, her mother told me, so I have invited her to watch our rehearsals."

Though I wanted to say how mortified Mother was over what she had said, and that my study of Greek had not taught me the difference between blood and fish, I was tongue-tied and muscle-bound. I had intended to say, "Thank you for letting me come," and then go back to where I had been sitting. I was unable to do either; the two men smiled at me abstractedly and there I stood. I think Miss Anglin understood that I did not know how to go away. She said, "Here comes Mr. Platt; I must talk to him about the *Iphigenia* costumes." It was a kind way of releasing and dismissing me. That night at dinner I told my family I had a delightful talk with Margaret Anglin, Livingstone Platt, the set and costume designer (I had overheard a member of the company tell another who he was) and two other gentlemen.

The next morning by nine o'clock I was back in the seat I had appropriated: I did not want to risk missing anything; the day before I had had nothing to eat until dinnertime. The second morning I brought lunch with me. That day I learned the play they were doing was Euripides' *Iphigenia in Aulis* and, from hearing their names called, I began to sort out some of the people involved. The two men whose base was on either side of Miss Anglin were Henry Hull, her husband—and I wondered how he had ever had the courage to aspire to such an honor—and Walter Damrosch, who, I found out later, had composed the incidental music for the plays. Carolyn Darling was Miss Anglin's secretary and also a member of the chorus. I thought her name exactly right because she came over, introduced herself and talked to me while I was having lunch. She said the man who told them what to do and where to stand, speaking in a heavy accent, was Gustav von Seyffertitz, an Austrian, and his title was director.

It was on the fourth or fifth day of my vigil that all of the Fourth of Julys in my life rolled into one simultaneously exploding pinwheel, Roman candle and skyrocket. Actually the day had not begun well. Mother had caught me as I was leaving the house. She had forgotten the night before, she said, to tell me they were all going across to the fair, spending the day. She knew I would not want to miss that. I think she was shaken by my boisterous outrage that anyone could think I wanted to do a childish thing like traipsing around a fair, when by special invitation I could be in a theater watching a play. She yielded; but I think she may have felt her authority slipping a little, because she made me go back to my room and write a letter to my father and one to my grandparents. So instead of being the first one at the theater I bolted in as red, hot and breathless as I had been on the first morning, and the company was already assembled. They were not on the stage, however; Miss Anglin was in her usual place and most of the others were standing near her, not talking. She saw me, unmistakably beckoned me to come to her, and I wished I were dead or had gone to the fair with my family. She had not spoken to or even noticed me since that first morning. Now she was going to tell me they did not want outsiders any more, or perhaps she had heard the noise of my coming and found it disturbing. I went to her thinking this was the last time I would see this wonderful place and these magic people until I came like everybody else to the performance.

"Emily," she said, when I had reached her, "we've had an accident this morning. One of our girls in the chorus fell and has sprained her ankle badly. I know you have been watching every day. Would you like to take her place in the chorus?"

That is the moment when inside me all the pinwheels, Roman candles and skyrockets exploded. Miss Anglin said later, considering to what lengths stagestruck young people would go in an effort to set foot in the theater, mine was an extraordinary invitation to appear on the stage, and mine was an unusual response.

"Oh, Miss Anglin," I told her, "if my family will let me." I did not know why everyone within hearing laughed.

"We will hope," Miss Anglin said gravely to the company, "they can be persuaded." Then briskly, "In the meantime, perhaps you would stand in. Carolyn, would you show her the place she's to take?"

As I followed Carolyn up the steps I remembered thinking if the family did not consent I would die but I would die at the summit of my life: I had stood on the stage in Margaret Anglin's company.

Permission did come but not easily and not without an aftertaste of bitterness. For nearly a week I did not tell Mother what I was doing because I thought a surprise announcement on the very day of the performance would be glorious, and also because I was afraid to ask; but on the morning it was announced that on the following Monday we would carry over to night rehearsals on through to the performance, I knew there was no postponing the surprise.

The moments of gratifying excitement at my news were brief; second thoughts followed immediately and they were dour. I was young, I would be in a group of older, far more sophisticated people, in a world apart. When I shouted I was neither young nor unsophisticated, I was told to keep quiet and let Mother think. The result of her thinking, after conferences with Aunt Lulie and the Boones, was a telegram to my father in Chicago, the first of a series of exchanges between them. When I was not at the theater I either cried or prayed. I did not dare say to anyone in the company I might not be allowed to stay. They had teased me in the beginning about my answer to Miss Anglin's invitation, but they thought I had said it out of embarrassment. By the end of the first day's work I had realized that for these people on their own, making a career, earning a living, any uncertainty about being allowed to do it was grotesque. Mother was sympathetic to this and when I told her to put herself in my place and try to see what it would be if I had to go to Miss Anglin and tell her, after days of training, I would have to drop out and they would have to start over again with someone new, she wrung her hands.

"I know, I know all that, Emily, don't think I don't understand but *you* don't understand." I know now that I didn't understand because to be fifteen in 1915 was to be very young, and to a family that had never touched its outer fringes, the theater was a glittering and dangerous world. For a girl who on school nights had supper at six and was in bed at eight-thirty, half past nine on Fridays and Saturdays, even physically this was a trial of strength.

The deciding telegram from my father came while I was at the theater. Mother was watching for me and came running down the path waving it above her head.

ALL THINGS CONSIDERED, it said, LET HER DO IT. TRUST YOUR JUDGMENT. GREAT EXPERIENCE FOR HER. ALL LOVE HAL.

"I think my last telegram did it," Mother told me with obvious satisfaction, after I had stopped yelling and waltzing her around. "I said since the plays were outdoors it would be very healthy for you."

There was the galling aftertaste that is with me today. A deciding factor in my going on the stage was not a great talent it would be wicked to deny, but that I would be in the fresh air. No one in Miss Anglin's company ever knew how brief my stay might have been and why it was not.

When the company was dismissed in the late afternoon of the day we were to have our first night rehearsal, Miss Anglin sent for me. She had not spoken to me except to include me in her good morning to everyone since the day of her invitation. She wanted to know where I was going to have supper. I told her Mother was coming and would bring it.

"That's all right then," she said. "But in the meantime"— she indicated a steamer rug on the chair beside her—"I want you to go up to the top of the theater away from everybody, wrap this around you and go to sleep. You can, you know, if you try. Anyone in the theater learns to go to sleep whenever there is a chance for it. Then you'll be fresh for the rehearsal tonight. It's very important in the theater, too, to take care of yourself; that's another thing you must learn."

I doubt I would have experienced in any other company such thoughtfulness from its star.

When I woke it was dusk. Mother was sitting not far from me and someone was singing. "Who is that?" I demanded, louder than I realized because I was startled and not yet awake.

"Hush," Mother told me. "It's Schubert." I had meant the singer, of course, and wide awake knew it was Merle Alcock. I had heard her lovely voice in solo passages of Mr. Damrosch's music. When I asked what part she played, I had been told she was not in the acting cast but would be on the program as a first soloist. Once she had spoken to me. With this superiority of acquaintanceship I unrolled quickly from my blanket and went over to introduce her to Mother. To my exasperated discomfiture, as I reached them Mother was saying, "And I will always remember your beautiful performance in *The Yellow Jacket*." Since I had also seen *The Yellow Jacket,* I might have said that too, instead of just simpering when she had spoken to me, except that it had never occurred to me this pretty woman could have been that Chinese mother.

There were no other soloists in the chorus so I do not

know why Merle Alcock was called the first one. As a group we would be moved on cue with specific gestures. Some of the members had speaking parts; the leader, Gertrude Wagner, had a long one. Once, generously, I was given a line but when "Death is the lot of all" was heard in my piping soprano, Miss Anglin said she had never heard a happier canary, and the line was quickly allotted to another maiden.

Mute, I was inconspicuously adequate in the chorus, or there was no one else available. At any rate, I was not asked to return to the benches and at the end of the first week I was paid. I still have the envelope with my name on it. I was not quite so levelheaded as to think everyone in the company was there for the pleasure of it, but I truly thought mine was an invitation generously given to an outsider. Actors' Equity was a new organization and its rulings were not recognized then. Certainly I had not heard of it and since the eighteen dollars in my pay envelope was larger by sixteen dollars and fifty cents than my weekly allowance, I would have considered daft anyone who wanted to improve working conditions in the theater. We rehearsed from ten in the morning until around midnight with pause for lunch and for dinner. I considered this an ideal schedule. I might have come out of my euphoric mist if I had heard around me any expressions of dissatisfaction. On the stage I was dumb because I could not speak a line convincingly, but I was not mentally backward nor was my hearing defective. In the intervals when we were not on the stage the members of the chorus talked and I listened. I learned about their families, their lodgings, their previous engagements, matters of love, but I never heard a protest about work and pay in the theater.

The work in the chorus consisted of specific movements on cues. Since from the first grade our school curriculum had included "aesthetic dancing" and eurythmics, I could follow directions without anxiety, though Mr. von Seyffertitz gave them in highly individual phrasing. One of his instructions is a favorite in my family to this day:

"I want you should move, young ladies, oh so leetle, almost hardly." He was punctiliously formal when he addressed the players but since he could not remember their names he would say:

"Mrs. Clytemnestra, may I ask you please to come on the stage and, Mr. Agamemnon, if you will stand here just so." However, I never heard him address Miss Anglin as Miss Iphigenia.

On the second of the night rehearsals Mother sent Hilda and Gertrude up the hill with supper for me. She thought they would enjoy watching a rehearsal. She also thought between them they could bring something more than sandwiches, milk and fruit for me since she had noticed, she said, how skimpily the people around her had been eating the night before. I do not remember what they brought that night in the basket they carried between them, but after that nothing could keep them from their nightly visit nor the feasts they provided. It was not love of the theater nor certainly of me that prompted this devotion. It was because Pedro de Cordoba, tall, dark, handsome, would station himself at the entrance to the theater and peering down through the eucalyptus trees begin his nightly call. That with some variations was:

"Do I hear the two most beautiful women in my life coming up the hill? How I love them, how I wait for the evening to be with them. Are they carrying between them a basket of beautiful things? Surely they will not let their own Pedro go hungry tonight."

Simpering, giggling, the two Scandinavians would come

in sight, panting and breathless under the weight of the basket that grew heavier each evening in direct proportion to the increase in Mr. de Cordoba's protestations of fervor and devotion. My own allotments from the provisions remained the same. Sometimes Mr. de Cordoba and his chosen group, among the more exalted members of the company, sent over to me and my humble associates a few tidbits.

Livingstone Platt's stage decorations were simple, classic and beautiful. High double gates in the center upstage marked the entrance to the palace of Agamemnon in the plays *Iphigenia* and *Electra,* and to the palace of Medea in that play; the costumes had far wider variety. The material was of a soft cotton crepe. This was dyed and, when the dye had set, was dampened and wrung as one would wring out a towel, then allowed to dry in tight folds. Released, it was like accordion pleating, soft and clinging. The colors were as soft as the texture, purple, lavender, magenta, rose, greens and orange. The costume was in two pieces: a basic straight shift from shoulder to heel; over this another layer of the material in a color contrasting to the shift was draped and it was not pleated. No two members of the chorus had the same arrangement of draping. Mr. Platt himself did each one individually. In our shifts and carrying our extra material we waited our turn, watching him create on the ones ahead of us an arrangement that would not be repeated. Sometimes an end trailed almost to the ground; on another girl it became a cowl with soft folds under the chin. Madam Fralick, the wardrobe mistress, stood beside him, holding a tray heavily loaded with safety pins of all sizes and strips of elastic of different lengths and widths, the kind of elastic—attached to a hat—from which I had recently and with vehemence been emancipated. The ones on Madam's tray were not to go under

the chin; these were put on like belts when Mr. Platt wanted to make a peplum or confine the whole draping in folds below the waist.

On the night of the *Iphigenia,* I was standing in line moving up to Mr. Platt when Carolyn Darling found me, with a message that Miss Anglin wanted to see me in her dressing room. Until that instant I had not felt the slightest nervous tremor. I am embarrassed to remember that; I must have been a clod or numb. I know that during the day, since there was no rehearsal, I had done unimportant things with the family, but there had been no talk of the play other than discussion of what time they should all start and a telephone call to the Boones to set a place for meeting. I have no recollection of saying to myself, "This is the greatest night of my life," nor having any anxiety about being at the proper place and with proper movements on cue.

When I left for the theater Mother had said, "With your shield or on it." She always said that on the day of examinations at school.

If my friends were not so casual and easygoing as usual when I joined them at the theater, I did not notice it. Someone told me to put on my shift, bring my drapery and wait in line for Mr. Platt. It had been more exciting the first time at the dress rehearsal the night before, but when Carolyn Darling told me Miss Anglin wanted to see me I knew panic. What had I done that was so awful Miss Anglin was going to dismiss me? Did she think I was so incompetent it was better for the performance to have nobody? Carolyn turned away from me to talk to the other girls, wishing them luck. She knew how nervous they were but they were going to be fine. Several of them said they had not been able to eat all day. One of them said she had thrown up three times and hoped the fourth wouldn't be on stage. This was why I was being dismissed, I decided. I had eaten at the usual time and the usual amount and had not in the least felt like throwing up. I had no temperament. I was sick now, not because I was going on the stage, but with the humiliation of leaving it, and the thought of my family coming to see me—and, of course, Miss Anglin and the play—and not finding me. I would certainly not wait for them after the play as Mother had planned. No skulking around for me, trying to keep out of sight; I would go home now or somewhere; perhaps I would never go home.

Carolyn said, "Coming, Emily?" I wanted to say good-bye to the others, thank them for being so nice to me, but I could not make sounds. I looked back at the door; no one had noticed my going.

Miss Anglin was at her dressing table.

"Come over here, Emily," she said, "and stoop down. No, I think it would be better if you got on your knees here in front of me." Flat on the floor was where I wanted to be. "That will be an easier height for me."

She turned away from her dressing table and reached for a tube that was on it.

"It suddenly came to me you wouldn't know the first thing about making up, so I thought I'd better do it. Now then, put your chin up a little so the light is better."

No one noticed when I came back to the chorus dressing room. Mr. Platt was draping the last girl. I took her place when he had finished. The world was beautiful; I was beautiful. I wondered did anyone recognize this ravishing creature I had just seen in Miss Anglin's mirror? I could not speak about the terrible thing that had almost happened to me and the wonderful thing that had happened, but I needed to talk.

"Oh, Mr. Platt," I said, and shivered extravagantly, "it's going to be cold out there tonight. Just listen to that wind."

Mr. Platt sat back on his heels and took a safety pin from his mouth.

"Child," he said, "that's the most beautiful sound in the theater; and for people in the theater," he added, "the most beautiful sound in the world. That's not wind, it's people, fourteen thousand of them, come to see you."

Then it broke over me, as if I had been knocked down by a giant wave; strangling, I gasped for breath. This was not the gymnasium of Miss Faulkner's School for Girls in Chicago, filled on an evening with parents and friends brought by duty and loyalty. Of the fourteen thousand people out there whose rustling movements came to us like a high wind, mine was probably the only parent of all of us who in a few moments would be on that stage. It was Theater that brought them. For two hours they would be lifted, carried up from their own world; they would be surprised and a little bewildered when they first returned to it. Long afterward they would say, "On such and such a night I saw Margaret Anglin in her production of *Iphigenia* and I will never forget it."

Certainly in that moment of strangulation I was not shaping this realization coherently, but I was whispering, and I remember it, "This is the theater and I'm in it." I also remember with equal clarity, the realization scared me witless. Compared with it my despair over Miss Anglin's summons was a shrug.

Mr. Platt finished draping me, called cheerily to all of us he knew we would do him proud. Mr. von Seyffertitz shook hands with him in the doorway telling him how stunning the set looked and called to us good luck and a laughing admonition to remember all the "leetle things." The door closed behind them on a silent room where we waited. No one was talking about being sick, or being sick. Gertrude Wagner, the leader of the chorus, crossed the room from the makeup table at which she had been sitting with her head in her hands, opened the door a crack. At the same moment the callboy said through it, "Overture." I had learned only a few minutes before, the title "callboy" and his purpose.

On that instant the wind outside dropped to scarcely a breath. Walter Damrosch was on the podium; his music began. We heard the passage for flute, piercingly sweet. We tiptoed out of our room to watch Merle Alcock pass us in the wings and move with exactly timed grace. As the lights came up slowly she sang the prologue to the play. No amplifiers distorted the beauty of her voice; its pure clarity rose without effort to the highest row in the theater. Mr. von Seyffertitz's direction had forestalled any interruption by applause. His Mr. Agamemnon, on the program identified as A. Fuller Mellish, and Paul Harvey, as Aegisthos, came through the gateway from Agamemnon's palace on the second the song ended. An involuntary spasm of applause was stopped immediately. For us in the wings the most important moment in the play was coming closer. We moved silently into position. Gertrude Wagner looked quietly back to see if we were all in place, gave a nod and led us from our hiding place backstage outside, around the rim of the theater nearest us and the stage, but not yet onstage. Her timing was so exact, at the moment we reached our starting point the orchestra gave us our cue, and the twenty maidens of Calchis flowed down the ramp and up the center stairs onto the stage. For me, at that moment, the play began.

The San Francisco *Chronicle*'s report of the performance said: "Flourish of trumpets preceded the cry 'Iphigenia is coming!' The music denoted the approach of Queen Clytemnestra and her daughter; the trumpeting and the shouting came nearer and the effect was carried on magnificent crescendo until through the southern gate the cavalcade appeared. Slaves marched down the ramp to the front of the amphitheater's broad stage, archers followed, then the soldiers bearing lances. Wedding gifts and bright arrayment were carried by a score of attendants. When the thrill of the spectacle was at its height, a chariot drawn by four horses abreast brought Clytemnestra and Iphigenia upon the scene. It was an entry full of life and spirit, splendidly dramatic in the climax." (I had thought this entrance anticlimactic to ours.) The paper also said: "There was not a seat nor even standing room available. It was the largest audience in the history of the Greek Theater."

I had heard the sound of it.

Medea was the next play. When I was told what hour to report for the first rehearsal my heart felt several pounds lighter and I was less disagreeable at home. I was no longer a substitute but actually a member of the company. There was a difference too in the others, a difference, that is, toward me. I had been a sort of kid sister treated with affectionate tolerance, though I doubt that any one of them was more than five years older than I. In 1915 the width between the ages of fifteen and twenty was a generation gap and from a nonprofessional family the distance to the country of the theater was as far as Spain from the beach of Atlantic City. To the featured players I was identified without a name as a good provider at suppertime. After night rehearsals or a performance, I knew they all gathered somewhere before they went home, and that many of them lived in the same boardinghouse. I loved to hear them talk about it. I went home with Hilda and Gertrude or Mother.

Everything changed when the *Medea* began. People called

me by my own name, Emily; it took me a long time to have the courage to say theirs. Mr. Platt asked me—I never called *him* Livingston—to help paint Medea's chariot; he would leave a dab of the proper color on each part of it, and give me the tins of paint. I doubt that Hebe bearing a cup for the first time felt more exalted. I had read the *Medea* so many times I knew it almost word for word, including the directions, and among those were: "Medea appears above the house in a chariot drawn by dragons. She has the dead bodies of the children with her." Medea, Margaret Anglin, would stand in a chariot painted by Emily Kimbrough. I was discomfited to find the masterpiece was not to be entirely my own artistry. But when the person Mr. Platt said would paint with me turned out to be a man, an "older man" who played one of the two messengers in the *Iphigenia*, I was reconciled to a degree of simpering pleasure. The term "older man" must not be confused with an "old man." To a fifteen-year-old, an older man was over eighteen and under thirty; beyond that he was old. This older man and I talked as we painted. One day when I told him, since there was no rehearsal called, I was going that evening with Mother to see the Exposition at night, he asked if he might come too.

We met by agreement at the ferry and I introduced him to Mother. He talked more to her than to me. It did not occur to me he might have found her the more interesting. I thought it was because I stayed apart from them; I was mortified because he did not wear a hat. When I asked if he had forgotten it, he looked surprised at my concern and told me he didn't own a hat. I pondered this as he and Mother talked and I reached two decisions: that if you were in the theater you were not like other people and you showed it, and until I found a way of my own I would copy my friends and not wear a hat again to the Exposition so that everyone there would know I was an actress.

A few days after this trip and my decision, Howard Lindsay, the assistant director, came to the theater with a hat he said he had gone to San Francisco to find. He was jubilant with success; I was dumbfounded. I had never seen a hat like it nor even a picture of one. I reasoned he wanted to look "different" too, but since he was not an actor, he could not be without one; perhaps to wear this would identify him as a director. When he saw my bewilderment he told me the hat was called a topee and was made for explorers and other people who were not natives in tropical climates, to protect them from the sun. He must have sensed I was looking at him with awe and I was, thinking I had never dreamed I would ever be talking to one person who was both a theater man and an explorer. He said quickly he was not going on any exploration. He and I were going to do a special job for Miss Anglin. The pith helmet was part of the equipment he had bought for it. Miss Anglin would tell me; would I please go to see her about it?

"I want literal translations of some of the passages in the play," she told me. "Just for my own study. I'm sure you can do this. I remember what your mother told me." She smiled and I, immersed in a beet-red blush, thought about matricide.

"Howard Lindsay can translate Greek too, so I would appreciate it very much if you would work together. I have shown him the passages I want."

We worked at the top of the theater away from everyone. Mr. Lindsay had bought two copies of the *Medea* in Greek, a dictionary, a trot, a long yellow writing pad, pencils and the topee. Since there was no place for us backstage where we could work in the shade undisturbed and without bothering other people, we would have to work in the open theater, on the top row to be by ourselves. He was taking precautions, because he was very sensitive to the sun.

The selection of topees could not have been wide because the one he had bought was several sizes larger than his head. In addition to my copy of the text open on my lap, I kept beside me a dictionary and the trot. Mr. Lindsay with the text had the long yellow writing pad. He kept the book open on his knees, the writing pad and pencil on the seat beside him. His right hand was free but he used the forefinger of his left to hold up the topee. He was a friendly, warm, charming but impatient man. He cleared away immediately most of my shyness, told me to forget he was a director and for heaven's sake call him Howard. A minute later, while I was looking up a word, he shouted a plea to God to explain why it took me so long; surely I must know the alphabet. His further objurgations were muffled because, reaching across to take the dictionary from my hands, he released the prop of his index finger and the pith helmet fell over his face. Its fall was swifter than its replacement; getting it back over the promontories of ears and nose was accomplished with tender care, and the descent always snuffed out his irascibility. When the contemplative pose—forefinger to the brow—was resumed his affability was restored. I can say this "always" occurred because the first time it happened evidently gave him no suggestion of how to avoid a recurrence. He neither removed the helmet nor took over the dictionary nor exercised patience; but we made and delivered to Miss Anglin the translations. I do not know how much they benefited her. They did not benefit me. Four years later at college, an examination set by my Greek professor included some of those passages. I failed the examination.

Recognition of Howard Lindsay as one of the most distingushed playwrights and actors of our time did not come to him by way of translations. Nevertheless, when I saw him and his wife, Dorothy Stickney, in the immortal *Life with Father,* I recognized nostalgically the irascibility that gave authority to his interpretation of the role of Father. As in "The Hunting of the Snark," "I skip forty years"; actually, perhaps half that number. Howard Lindsay had moved up steadily and brilliantly in the world of the theater. I had been in the obscurity of education and jobs unrelated to the theater. Our paths came together again on a book I had written. The difference in age had been closed as always happens by the stitches of time; he and Dorothy became my dear friends. Talking one day of Howard's portrayal of Father, Dorothy explained, "He's not a *bad*-tempered man, he's *quick*-tempered." And that, I thought, was exactly the right translation of Howard. "I skip forty years" or half that number back to the summer of 1915.

One morning a week before the performance of *Medea* I came into a nearly silent theater. Always before reaching the top of the hill I had heard sounds of activity that made me run the last part of the way lest I be missing something. That morning I had run because there were no sounds. No carpenters sawing and banging bits of scenery or whatever required carpentry, no electricians calling out their technical jargon to one another, no bellowing summons for Livingstone Platt or Mr. von Seyffertitz or Howard Lindsay, nor the buzz of actors passing the time of day until the call of "Places, please" would silence everyone. I knew I was not late enough for that call to have been given. I wondered if there was to be no rehearsal that day and I had not been told. I was running when I came through the entrance and stopped because everyone seemed to be there and no one seemed to be talking. There were three groups of people: Miss Anglin, surrounded by the important ones, the lesser members of the cast with the chorus, and at a little distance from both, the working staff. I was even more bewildered to see Madam Fralick, the wardrobe mistress, and the only woman among the mechanics; I had never before seen her out front, even at a dress rehearsal. What made it become frightening to me was that there was no audible sound coming from any of these people. I could see Miss Anglin speaking and the people around her answering and talking among themselves with an occasional gesture. Their voices were so low no sound of them reached me. I went, probably on tiptoe, to my own group; I know I whispered to the girl I reached first.

"What's the matter? Has something happened?"

"Has something happened?" she echoed. "Only that the Messenger fell on the ramp this morning. He's been taken to the hospital; we're waiting to hear how badly he's hurt." We had all fallen into Mr. von Seyffertitz's habit of calling the actors by their play names. I suppose to make sure this appalling news was true and we were talking about the same person, I said, "You mean Pedro de Cordoba?" They were all listening; several of them nodded, one of them added:

"He came early, to work on his entrance in the big scene running down the ramp, saying his opening lines."

"He told me"—another one spoke up—"he told me yesterday he wasn't satisfied with the timing of the running and the speaking. He wanted to speed it up. He said it had to come all in a rush."

"I don't understand why he fell," someone else said.

"Probably had on rubber shoes like Margie." This was Lucille Evans speaking and she turned to me. "She's the girl who had your place and got hurt on the ramp."

A man came out on the stage from somewhere in the back. I had thought no one was left there. He spoke as he walked forward.

"It's the hospital calling Miss Anglin."

Miss Anglin jumped from her chair but Howard Lindsay put his hand on her arm. "I'll take it, Miss Anglin," he said. She did not persist. She sat down again immediately. "If you would, Howard, thank you."

One of the girls behind me said, "She hasn't the strength to go. She's so afraid of what they may tell her." I am sure no one spoke in the next few minutes; I know there was complete silence when Howard came from the back and walked across the stage, down the steps and to Miss Anglin. He made no effort to lower his voice.

"It's bad," he said. We all heard him. "Compound fracture."

Someone gave a long, low whistle; there was no other audible sound. Everyone was certainly, like me, counting over in his mind the implications and ramifications of this announcement—pain, hospitalizing and weeks of inactivity for Pedro de Cordoba; disaster for the play. In 1915 a replacement could not be flown out from New York. Geographically Hollywood was nearer than New York but it was just a place then. Miss Anglin interrupted the silence with a laugh that was forced, and not gay.

"Now if this were only happening in a play," she said, "someone of you would rise up at this point and say, 'I know the part, let me play it,' but—"

A young man from our group stood up; my friend, the one who did not own a hat. He shuffled his feet, coughed, made a few *eh* sounds and finally said in a rush of words, "I do happen to know the part, that is, most of it. I don't know if you'd consider letting me—" What he said was like a fresh wind blowing; we were out of the doldrums. Miss Anglin jumped to her feet and everyone followed.

"Take your places, please." She reached the center steps and stopped. "No, I'll watch. Carolyn, take over for me." She went back to her seat. Mr. Damrosch must have joined her. I did not notice then.

My friend went up the ramp, the chorus on the stage divided into the grouping for that scene. Carolyn Darling, in Miss Anglin's place, came through the great doors, stood on the first of the steps leading down from the palace. Miss Anglin called, "Now."

Down the ramp the Messenger came in wild panic flight, like an animal stampeding from death, but over the noise of his feet a voice of horror reached us. We had not heard the like of it.

"Get thee away, Medea, get thee away. Fly." Then he was up the steps to the stage, spilling out to her the dreadful recital of the death of the princess, Jason's bride, from the poisoned robe Medea had sent as a wedding gift, brought to her by Medea's and Jason's two children; and the death of the king, father of the princess, when he had knelt, "and groaning low, folded her in his arms and kissed her," and been himself enmeshed in the robe. "And there they sleep at last, the old proud father and the bride."

In that scene, we in the chorus knew exactly what we must do, each move to make, each word in the Messenger's speech that was our cue. From the moment the hair-raising yell of "Get thee away, Medea" had reached us, not one of us stirred. We were frozen in our places.

When the scene ended and we realized we were breathing again, with a quick glance from one to another we knew what we had failed to do; but on the instant we were all

144

of us turning to look down at Miss Anglin. She was staring at the Messenger, smiling tremulously, shaking her head as if in wonder.

"The part is yours, of course," she said, "but you've brought a moment in the theater I think not one of us will ever forget."

Mr. Damrosch stood up. He had been sitting beside her. He walked over across the ramp, stood below the stage to one side of the steps. He reached up his hand.

"Young man," he said, "tell me your name. I want to thank you for a great experience, and I have known a few."

The young man came to the lip of the stage, squatted awkwardly on his haunches, stretched his hand down. I thought how big it was and saw his face and neck were fiery red. He reached Mr. Damrosch's hand with his own.

"Why, thank you very much, sir. My name is Alfred Lunt."

Postscript: That autumn I was sent to boarding school, to Miss Wright's School in Bryn Mawr, Pennsylvania. During the winter Alfred Lunt came to Philadelphia in *The Country Cousin,* by Booth Tarkington, starring Alexandra Carlisle. I had not been reticent about my stage experience and my friends in "the profession," but when Miss Wright told me I was to be sent in to a matinee as a special treat, so that I might see my friend, I wished God would punish me for boasting, by striking me dead. When Alfred Lunt was the Messenger, I had been a member of the chorus. When I went to see Alfred Lunt in *The Country Cousin,* I was in the school uniform of a blue serge sailor suit, called a Peter Thompson, and I was accompanied by a chaperon, Miss Janney, my English teacher. Prodded by her, I had to send backstage my name and a request to see him after the performance. We went back, I hoping at each step I could run away, but I did not; I only stood mute, wet-handed, unable to answer his polite inquiries about my present activities, because I was afraid I would vomit. Miss Janney filled a ghastly silence.

"Mr. Lunt," she said, "I have brought an invitation from Miss Wright, and this is a surprise to Emily, a treat for her and for all of us. Miss Wright would be happy to have you as a guest of the school on Sunday afternoon at our Evensong."

For one beautiful instant, there was a flash of understanding in a look he gave me across Miss Janney, and I answered it. He regretted that because of another engagement he must forgo the pleasure of such an occasion. I have seen him very infrequently since that day. I am sure he forgot it years ago. I will never forget it and I never forgave Miss Wright and Miss Janney.

VIII

Homecoming

The evening of the day the mail had brought Mr. Johnson's letter about Margaret Anglin, I had dinner with Katharine Cornell at her house. She has been a cherished friend for more years than we can remember. I told her about the letter.

"All day I've been reliving that summer. I dug up from my storeroom in the basement an album of photographs taken then. The back of the album was off. I'm going to have it rebound."

Kit urged me to tell her about the summer, not the album, but I would not be persuaded.

"Too long for telling now, but I'm going to write it and," I added, "the story of your opening night in Buffalo in *A Bill of Divorcement.*"

This obviously startled her. She began sentences and interrupted herself. "What on earth made you think of—Why would you—?"

"Because," I cut in, "I always seem to think, at least to remember, in pairs. When I thought about the night of *Iphigenia*, I almost immediately remembered the night of the *Bill of Divorcement* opening. They were great experiences in the theater—separate but equal—so I connected them."

Kit shook her head ruefully and laughed. "I didn't know you were there."

Her laughter surprised me as much as evidently I had surprised her. "In the whole evening," I said, "there was nothing to laugh at, though Lord knows it was joyous."

"You tell me how it was for you," Kit suggested, snuggling into the cushions of her chair like a child waiting for a bedtime story, "and then I'll tell you why I laughed."

To set the stage a little, I told her about my family's moving from Chicago to Buffalo because of a postwar reorganization in my father's factory at North Tonawanda that we both know is under an hour's distance from Buffalo. The stay was to be temporary, but in my dour anticipation a week was too long a duration, so I had spent as little time there as possible, going for holidays from college, except at Christmas, on visits. When college was finished and some family coercion had been applied, I came to Buffalo, where I did not know anyone and was positive I never would. I could not have been more mistaken. "I did make friends, have gay times, and I never met anywhere a more attractive group."

Kit nodded. "Buffalo people are like that, when you know them."

"You and I can never remember where we met and through whom, but I can't imagine why, until now, we've never talked about that night." My friend urged me to stop speculating and get on with it. I obliged.

"Well, I did make friends. I even collected a few beaus and one of them, Jack Sprague, invited me to go with him to the opening night of *A Bill of Divorcement.*

"The moment it was announced the play was coming to

Buffalo, I began hearing about you. Everywhere I went people talked about Kit coming and who Kit was and how she was tops in sports, tops evidently in everything, until I began to be a little bit irked about the one and only Kit. I wasn't irked, but I was surprised, when Jack told me everyone would wear evening clothes to your opening. I'd been to the theater in Buffalo and I'd never seen an audience there in evening clothes. I knew your father owned the theater; there were few things I hadn't been told in the incessant conversations about you. You had recently married but in Canada, and everyone was looking forward to meeting this Guthrie McClintic. So I thought this was the reason for our dressing; there was probably going to be a party, a belated wedding reception after the play.

"Jack was right about wearing evening clothes, but they were not evening clothes, I discovered, for a minor party. As the audience settled in, taking off coats, I saw many of the men were in white tie and tails; the women, dressed for a ball, were pulling up and smoothing long white gloves. Another thing that surprised me was the comparative silence of the audience. Usually people waved across the house or talked back and forth with friends in the row in front or in back. I had learned that, unlike Chicago or New York, Buffalo was a community in which you were bound to see friends in almost any audience and if it was a special event, as this one certainly was, practically everyone but me would know everyone else and be talking and calling across the floor, even up to the balcony.

"The curtain went up and I forgot about everything but the play. At the moment of your entrance, Jack whispered to me, 'There's Kit,' as if I didn't know, and from the silence around he must have been the only one in the audience who said anything. I had expected a crash of applause, stamping feet; I had even picked up my bag and program in my lap for a standing ovation. There was nothing, absolutely no recognition. I was so confounded I whispered back to Jack:

" 'You said Kit, didn't you?'

" 'Hush,' he said, or it may have been 'Shut up.' I know I was cowed by it.

"No one else came onstage who could possibly have been you and certainly I had looked at the program. I knew Janet Beecher was playing the part of your mother, Margaret Fairfield, and I had seen her before so I recognized her immediately. Allan Pollock was playing your father, Hillary Fairfield, but he had not come on as yet and anyway there would be small likelihood of my confusing you with *him*. I had not seen before the actress playing the part of Miss Hester Fairfield but I could not have mistaken that vinegared, tight-lipped, elderly spinster for you, and finally there you were on the program, Sydney Fairfield, Katharine Cornell. To clinch the whole thing your mother, Mrs. Fairfield, had gone to the foot of the stairs calling, 'Sydney darling, shall I bring up your coffee?' I remember the line to this day, and your voice answering. And then your appearance and dead silence from the audience.

"Well, the play went on and I was absorbed in it, paying no more attention to the apathy around me.

"When the curtain went down on the first act, Jack and I moved out with almost everyone else in the audience to the foyer. We joined a group of people we both knew. I was impatient with the usual round of hellos and how are yous and interrupted, 'Isn't she wonderful? Katharine Cornell, I mean, of course! What a voice, and how beautifully she moves.' There was a dead silence that was almost physical, as if I'd been slapped in the face. Someone broke it by saying Elizabeth and George Field were back in town, had anyone seen them? I was so embarrassed I moved off to another group. The same thing happened there. At the mention of your name, I was snubbed as if I had laughed aloud in the middle of a funeral, and the general atmosphere wasn't unlike one. People were talking in subdued tones and I didn't hear your name mentioned except by me; after my second attempt I was even more subdued than the rest of them seemed to be. I didn't speak to Jack again when we were back in our seats, and he showed no inclination to talk to me.

"We didn't go out in the intermission after the second act; I think very few people did; stragglers, nothing like the crush in the aisle we had worked our way through the time before, but I was so immersed in what had gone on on the stage I wanted only to think about it and Jack seemed disinclined again to talk, so I was not particularly aware of other people; but my impression is nearly everyone stayed. I did come out of my absorption enough to realize how still the house was all through the intermission, as it is usually only at the moment when the curtain goes up.

"The play moved into that inevitable heartbreaking end. As long as I live I will not forget your scene of renunciation of the boy you loved when you'd discovered there was insanity in your family; deliberately provoking him to quarrel, flouting him, accusing him of being in love with another girl and then when you sent him off bewildered, furious, calling after him impishly, 'You'll give her my love?' and when the door had slammed behind him, I'll never forget the change in your voice and that line of despair, 'You'll give her *my love.*' I don't cry easily and almost never in the theater, but that moment and the rest of the play undid me. I was wiping my eyes with a sodden wad of handkerchief when the curtain went down.

"When it went up again it was to something I've never seen the like of in the theater before nor since: sheer, glorious pandemonium from the audience. Every member of it was on his feet, certainly it was a standing ovation; it was a cheering, laughing, shouting paean-of-joy-and-pride demonstration. Old ladies around me were waving handkerchiefs and calling, 'Kit, dear, dear Kit.' Men were shouting. In the overall noise I couldn't hear what any of them were calling out except Carl Sprague, Jack's older brother, who was in the row ahead of us. He turned round to us, his back to the stage. 'Did you see the way she jumped over that couch?' he said, 'just the way she's always jumped into a canoe; never saw such balance in my life.' Tears were running down his face; he knew it and didn't care.

"Then *I* knew why all these people had been so strangely quiet between the acts, so remote during the intermission, abstracted as if they were thinking of something else, and why they had snubbed me when I mentioned your name. It was because you belonged to them, all of them. You were not an unknown little girl from the other side of the tracks. This was your circle, a closed one around you, and I was an outsider. This was your family, eager and apprehensive, dressed to do you honor, holding its breath until you should prove yourself and then pouring out its love and praise. You had come through with all they'd hoped for and they told you so. You remember when Allan Pollock came out to take a bow he brought you with him? I can see him now as he stood smiling understandingly at the tumultuous crowd and then with a little bow to you and a lovely wave of the arm

circling the audience and you, as if he were saying, though certainly he couldn't have been heard had he tried to say it, 'She belongs to you; I have no place here,' and he left the stage and you alone on it. I doubt that the audience saw any part of that; it was talking directly to you.

"I know I didn't meet you that night but I was longing to tell you some of these things I as an outsider realized. Jack and I went to a party. Nobody there talked of anything but the play and you but you weren't there. When I realized you were not coming, I decided that because I was a newcomer and outsider we had not been included in *the* party."

Kit shook her head. Her eyes were unnaturally bright at the moment. I think she was close to tears, remembering. She shook her head.

"I wasn't at that party," she said. "I wasn't at any party. I'll tell you the ending of that night and why I laughed." She smiled again. "Guthrie and I had not been in Buffalo since we were married and Guthrie had never been, so this was a double homecoming and double nervous excitement for me, I might add. Professionally and personally any opening is such anguish as to make you wish to God you'd never walked through a stage door. To give a performance to an audience with friends and family in it is double death.

"On top of that, if anything could top it, I was nervous about introducing Guthrie. I wanted everybody to feel a little the way I felt about him. I made an idiotic start in that direction. Guthrie was doing a play and could only get away for two days and only this by the insistence and double work of the company. Instead of being very touched and grateful, I was horrified to find he hadn't brought evening clothes. Poor darling, there was nothing in the world he hated more, and certainly it hadn't occurred to him to wear them to the theater. What with one thing and another, I was evidently hysterical in my insistence. It scared him so, he told me later, he promised he would get them, and wear them. You can imagine the telephoning: asking someone to dig them out and find a way to send them; this was the day before the opening. The solution was to put them on the night train in the care of the porter of the Buffalo car. The train got in around seven in the morning and he met it. You can imagine what that itself was to an actor. All I knew was that he had them and would wear them. So I could concentrate my hysteria on the play. You know this was my first big part; the only things I'd done before in Buffalo were bits in the Jessie Bonstelle repertoire company there and since my father owned the Majestic Theater, in which it played, I was just Dr. Cornell's little girl. This was my first chance to prove I was perhaps a little more than that. So you can imagine what this added to the inevitable opening night fever. Well, you were there, you know how it went off and of course the response at the end of the play was certainly something I'll never forget.

"When I finally got back to my dressing room, Guthrie was waiting there, so handsome in his evening clothes and so understanding of how overwhelmed I was. He was too, for that matter. I think I probably cried a little on his shoulder. I know I rushed then to get into my very best clothes that I'd brought down to the theater so that I could match him. I sent word that I was ready and Guthrie and I stood by the door like a receiving line.

"After a while we moved back into my room and sat down. We talked about moments of the play and made other conversation. I suppose it was perhaps an hour or so later, when we'd run out of talk anyway, that Guthrie said apologetically he was awfully sorry but he was afraid he would have to leave or he'd miss his night train back to New York.

"We got hold of a taxi somehow; there was no one around the theater when we came out. We went straight to the station; he had brought his bag down to the theater with him. I saw him to the train; I'd kept the taxi waiting and when he had left I drove home. No one was up. The maids had gone to bed and Father was at a party with his contemporaries. He'd taken it for granted, he said later, we were going somewhere with our own friends. I let myself in—I still had a key to the house—turned on the lights as I went through to the kitchen. I got a bottle of milk out of the icebox and found some crackers on the shelf. I sat down at the kitchen table and had the only food I had eaten that day. Then I went up to bed, read for a while and turned off the light.

"The next morning the telephone began ringing before eight o'clock and from then on it didn't stop. Every conversation began with something like, 'Darling, I knew you would be too tired after the performance to have to talk to people so, of course, we didn't go backstage, but I want to tell you . . .' Bless their hearts, they knew so little about the ways of the theater, it never occurred to them you're so keyed up after a performance it takes hours to unwind and that of all the nights in my life this was the one when I wanted my old friends around me and Guthrie." Kit laughed again reminiscently. "That's how the big night ended," she said.

IX

Of Relative Importance

One day last summer when we had finished the marketing list, Bessie said she must speak to me about something else. Bessie is my cook, housekeeper, friend, counselor, and I listen to her.

"It's about Eliza," she said. "She's got me worried. I think she needs straightening out. You'd better speak to her mother."

Eliza's mother is my daughter, with whom I enjoy speaking about a great many things, in which the bringing up of her children is not included. One reason for this abstention on my part is that I find her children delightful, congenial individuals, possessing too another quality that is perhaps old-fashioned of me to appreciate—good manners. Therefore it ill behooves me to make suggestions, let alone criticisms. A parent with any sense at all knows that after her child is married almost any suggestion unsolicited is ill behooving. Therefore I temporized with Bessie about Eliza. Eliza and a friend, Bitsy, each of them twelve years old, were spending two weeks with me at the seashore in Rhode Island. They were so self-sufficient, with so many projects, I had seen very little of them except at shared games in the evening. I wondered uneasily if I had exercised sufficient supervision.

"If they've been bothering you," I suggested, "I'll tell them to stay out of the kitchen." Bessie protested this.

"They don't bother me. I like having them there. You wouldn't find nicer little girls, but Eliza needs talking to. This morning I was fixing the breakfast trays. They were helping me. Bitsy seemed to know exactly what to do, but Eliza had to be told everything, so I said to her, 'Eliza, you look at Bitsy how she knows her way around the kitchen. She's going to be a wonderful wife one of these days but you better watch out and learn a few things or you'll never get a husband.' And do you know what she said to me? She said, 'Bessie, you don't have to worry about that at all. I don't have to know about these things, because I'm going to marry a horse.'"

When I had left Bessie in the kitchen, reassured that the possibility of such miscegenation was not immediate, I allowed myself a modest cavorting in the back hall. As recently as the day she had brought Eliza and Bitsy, my daughter had made reference to the shocking ignorance of sex among the youth of my generation, contrasting it with the perhaps too easy familiarity of the present.

"Eliza and our two boys," she had said, "have known everything since they were five years old. What her approach to it will be at the age of, say, sixteen or seventeen, I just don't know."

More immediately than at sixteen a few vital statistics would have to be inserted into Eliza's range of knowledge. The happy prospect of telling my daughter this had prompted the previous moment's skittishness. Sobriety returning, I knew my daughter's thoroughness. Eliza undoubtedly at some point had stopped listening, retaining only what at the time had seemed interesting. I remembered then a plaintive admission Stephen Benét had made to me when his children and mine were small. Rosemary, their mother, had decided the time had come for imparting this knowledge and insisted Stephen should bestow it. When Rosemary Benét was Rosemary Carr and I was eleven years old, we had become friends. I knew her gentleness, sweetness, warmth—and strength of purpose.

"So one evening," Stephen had told me, "after I'd rehearsed for a week what I was going to say, sweating over it as much as over anything I've ever written, I told them the 'facts,' and do you know what's happened?" When Stephen expressed astonishment, his eyes behind his glasses seemed literally to grow half again their usual size. "It's turned out to be their favorite bedtime story. So now I have to tell it over and over. They make me skip some parts. We've cut out the bees and flowers completely."

When my daughter A, Eliza's mother, was ten years old, she delivered our miniature poodle, Sarah, of four puppies. In my program of education in the "facts," this event had not been intended as an object lesson. It was to have taken place some days later at the vet's. Confident of the date, I had gone to New York. A's twin sister, B, after a siege of illness, was at school for the winter in Arizona. Other than A, Sarah and her approaching family, the only other occupants of the house were Bertha, the cook, and Mary, the waitress, who was timid.

Over the telephone in about the middle of the night, I had the first news of the accouchement from A, who burst into tears during her joyous recital. When I had persuaded her to relinquish the telephone to Bertha, I gave instructions of bed with a hot water bottle, aspirin, sleeping late, no school, and I caught an early-morning train home. A was in good health and spirits, Sarah and the puppies were in splendid condition.

Bertha seemed a bit haggard. She filled in parts of the story A's tears had blurred. She had been asleep when A had run down the back hall and pounded on her door, telling her to get up quickly and help her, Sarah was having puppies. Mary had heard her too and, according to her own story, at the news had got out of bed, bolted the door and gone back with the covers over her head.

Bertha had flung on a robe, met A in the hall. "That child knew what she was doing, so I just minded what she said. She was the general. She told me to go down to the kitchen and boil a kettle of water, so that's what I did."

A's story, more coherently told than on the night before, was that she had been wakened in her room next to mine by "funny noises" in my room. She had promptly and typically investigated. In her life, A has never locked a door and gone back to bed with the covers over her head. She had found Sarah on my bed and, watching her, was alarmed. Using the telephone on my night table, she had immediately called Dr. Ivens, the vet. Holding the telephone, she said, in one hand and patting Sarah with the other, while she described the dog's symptoms, she had burst out, the doctor said later, like a popgun the minute the telephone was answered. He had interrupted her.

"Now listen to me, A," he had said. "This is Dr. Ivens, Sr. Bill's out on a case and you know I can't come to you." She knew Dr. Ivens, Sr., had given up practice after a heart attack.

"Now I'll tell you exactly what's the matter with Sarah and what you're going to do. Sarah is going to have puppies, and you're going to help her."

She had repeated his instructions back to him before she

hung up the telephone and had immediately called Bertha.

"He told me," was A's recital, "to sterilize a pair of scissors in boiling water, so I told Bertha to make some. He said get a box of some kind. There wasn't any in your bedroom and I didn't want to leave her, so I dumped your hats out and took that one. I filled the hot water bottle only a little bit, the way Dr. Ivens told me, put it on the bottom of the hatbox and folded a bath towel on top of it. I yelled to Bertha to bring me up some newspapers and I lifted Sarah up and put them underneath her. She didn't want to get off the bed and I didn't know where else to put her anyway."

To my bewilderment, A seemed not so impressed by the arrival of the puppies as by the importance of the things she herself must do.

"He said the puppy would come in a little sac and mostly the mother would know to bite it open and tear it off, but maybe Sarah wouldn't because this was her first litter, she might be nervous. If she didn't, I should crook my first finger, hook it in enough to break the sac but not too deep and then peel it off myself, and I did. He said there would be a long cord attached from the puppy's stomach to Sarah's. If she didn't bite it off, I was to cut it, not too long and not too short—that's what the scissors were for! He told me how to measure it against my own finger. And that's what I did. Then I gave the puppy to Sarah. She licked it and licked it and pushed it from one side to the other, but I wasn't scared because Dr. Ivens said that was what she would do until the little puppy began to squeal. Then I took it away and put it on the bath towel in the hatbox. I wanted to see if it was a boy or a girl but I guess I was so excited I couldn't really tell. Of course I knew where to find out. Bertha said it was a boy. I took off the sacs and cut the cords for each of them;

Sarah seemed to want me to do it. When Bertha and I were sure there weren't going to be any more, we took the puppies out of the box and gave them to Sarah. She knew exactly what to do then and the puppies did too. It was just wonderful. After that I called up Dr. Ivens and told him all about it. Dr. Ivens, Jr., had just come in, so he came on the telephone and I told him too and he said he didn't believe he needed to come over at all; I had done everything. I don't think I got quite enough newspapers on your bed. I'm sorry about that."

When I had given wholehearted praise of her competence and steadiness, I told her a very special part of the experience had been that she had actually seen what I had told her and B about the way *they* were born.

A looked at me severely. "Well," she said, "I hope *you* had sense enough to take off the sac and bite the cord; after all, it was your first litter."

B's response to my explanation of how mothers nurse their babies I have not forgotten either. B's questions were always practical and pertinent.

"Is there cream on top?" she asked.

Stephen Benét's assertion of selection I can corroborate. My children selected to remember only the parts that interested them and frequently rejected an explanation given, preferring one of their devising. Sensing an unexpressed preference, I sometimes answered with wild inaccuracy; I carry no sense of guilt about it. One night when the twins had been put to bed and I was dressing to go out to dinner B had called me time and again to her room, telling and asking me trivia in a desperate effort, I knew, to push off the bleak isolation of waiting for sleep. When with finality I called back there must be no more summonses, she begged urgently for just one more question and certainly I yielded. Looking up at me as I stood beside her bed, fastening my dress, she asked:

"Mommy, when you and I were born together in a hospital, did the sheep and the cows move over to make room for us?"

"Yes," I said, "that's just exactly how it was. Now go to sleep."

When I looked in five minutes later on my way to the party, she was in sweet untroubled slumber. She had selected a way in which she wanted to be born and had only wanted corroboration. It had not been an appropriate moment for enlightenment.

Selectivity, undoubtedly, was responsible for my deplorable ignorance, when I entered college, of the basics in sex. Since Mother, who died when she was only forty-eight years old, is not here to defend herself, I cannot dishonor her by an assertion that "she never told me." Disliking with contempt any sentimentality, she would not have swaddled the facts of life into cotton-batting obscurity. Undoubtedly I chose to remember what interested me. My absorption was in birth, not what preceded it. A seed was planted and from then on interesting things happened.

The only even vague speculation I remember occurred one day in eighth-grade Latin class when I asked Miss Faulkner what a bastard was. She told me to look it up. I said I had looked it up and the definition was "illegal." That, I knew, meant against the law; I did not see the connection. Miss Faulkner, obviously hedging, said she did not want to take up the time of the class in explanation. Would I ask my mother to tell me?

Mother said a bastard was a baby whose parents were not married to each other and that was against the law. She added a law of her own making. When I came upon a word like that I was not to introduce it in class; I was either to wait until I got home and ask her or at least to wait until the class was dismissed and ask the teacher. There were things that were better discussed privately. At some time after that, in ancient history class, I had felt a need to know more about a word used in the textbook. The sound of it suggested to me kinship with "bastard." Observing Mother's law, I asked Miss Boyce if I could speak to her after class. When the room was empty—Miss Boyce reminded me of it many years later —I had stood on tiptoe, whispered into her ear, "What is a roisterer?" She had told me a roisterer was a bully, someone who was a troublemaker.

I formed my own kinship between the two: bastards were produced by roisterers. Whatever the means was of no consequence.

Science was not a college entrance requirement. I took advantage of this in my determination to avoid biology, the one science course offered at school. I wanted no part in cutting up frogs. Even had I taken it, I might not have been enlightened about basic structure, because my contemporaries have told me the vital parts were omitted in textbooks then.

In my freshman year at college a lecture was given, extracurricular but compulsory, under the title "Hygiene." The lecturer was a maiden lady of frightening convictions. She told us nothing anatomical, but she thundered to our astonishment an awful responsibility we must recognize and carry. A youth's unsullied progress to manhood was jeopardized whenever he danced with a girl who was wearing a dress of georgette or chiffon. Many a man whose life ended in the gutter could thank for the beginning of his downfall a dancing partner in a chiffon dress. After a foxtrot or one-step

with a Bryn Mawr, Smith or Vassar houri, the distraught young man went from the ballroom straight to hell.

This appalling revelation scared most of us out of sanity. For months, the weekend following that lecture had been marked jubilantly on the calendars of the favored ones who had bids to the Princeton prom.

After the lecture, contrary to custom, my group of friends did not meet in what we called "soul scrapes" to make our decisions. Each of us struggled privately with her conscience and the future of young manhood, because each of us had a chiffon or georgette dress. The result was a spate of telegrams like a snowfall, each carrying a message in one form or another that due to unforeseen circumstances she could not come to the prom. When the young men telephoned irascibly to demand the reason for their being "stood up," we could not of course tell them it was for their own good. Meeting one another dismally on our own campus that weekend, we tried to find comfort in our nobility and our martyrdom. Only one was absent from the melancholy scene, a girl named Frances Jones, and called Jonesy. Jonesy, we learned, had been saddled by her parents with a taffeta dress. Following the lecture she had gone straight in to Philadelphia, purchased at Wanamaker's a flame-colored chiffon and headed for Princeton on Friday afternoon.

Jonesy had beaus. We all wanted them; not Jonesy's, just ours. In Freshman Show we sang a song that began, "I want to have a beau of my own, Before all beaus are gone." With some variations, it was like making a stamp collection, only we called them "scalps." No village postmistress knew better the correspondence in her community than we in a dormitory, scanning the mail table, knew that the morning a letter postmarked New Haven came to the girl who up to then was including Cambridge, Princeton, Amherst and Williamstown in a week's allotment of mail, that girl had acquired another scalp. In theater vocabulary a heavy is the villain; in ours a heavy was a suitor who was serious.

Jonesy's mail was fat and widespread. She admitted her success and attributed it to her line. A girl who did not have a line was a flop, a prune. She could have a soft line or a sweet one; some even had a speedy line. Without one or another of these she might better stay at college and be a greasy grind.

In the pursuit of beaus, the current saying was, "A Bryn Mawr girl says, 'How much does he know?'; a Vassar girl says, 'How much has he got?'; a Wellesley girl says, 'Who is he?'; and a Smith girl says, 'Where is he?'"

Smarting under this classification, girls from Bryn Mawr exacted a promise from the beau who had asked her to a prom never to say Bryn Mawr, but to tell his friends his girl was at a school outside Philadelphia.

Jonesy, in the winter of our freshman year, with business acumen, capitalized on her recognized success by giving lessons in a line. On her door she tacked a long sheet of yellow-lined paper from a writing pad, marking the hours when she would be available and leaving spaces between for applicants. I doubt that any signature appeared more frequently than mine. She charged twenty-five cents a lesson, and to squeeze that much out of my allowance for several lessons a week meant forgoing all fudge sundaes and mocha cake in the village. My teacher reclined on a window seat in her room, an open box of candy beside her, and on a table within easy reach a Victrola. The candy was, of course, from one of her scalps. Between directions and watching her pupil she nibbled a bonbon held in a pair of silver tongs. I wore my hockey uniform because I always came immediately after athletics period. The component parts of the uniform were a white middy blouse, blue serge bloomers, black-ribbed heavy cotton tights and black gym shoes. The hockey stick I held in front of me was my dancing partner.

After telling me what I should say and how to say it, Jonesy would start the Victrola and I with my hockey stick would move into a foxtrot or whatever the music required. Dancing was easy. I loved it, but that was not enough and I knew it. At the count of one, Jonesy taught me, I lowered my head, saying simultaneously, "No," in a tone of astonishment; held my head down, for the count two, three, four;

raised it; opened my eyes wide, and said, "Really?" on an up inflection of amazement. She wanted me to open my mouth a little when I looked up. I practiced it over and over but she made me cut that part.

"You open it too wide," she said. "It's supposed to be alluring. You look moronic."

Round and round the room. "No," two, three, four, "Really?," two, three, four. Then I could go on dancing with the assurance that my partner, responding to my breathless interest, would tell me more. When there were indications of his running down, I was to revive him quickly with "No," two, three, four, "Really?," two, three, four. There were variations on this but the clincher was a repartee Jonesy guaranteed to be surefire. She would have to charge a dollar to reveal and teach it. I bought it by washing another girl's hair for a dollar. The dollar revelation was, "You're so big and strong," and you were to say it as if you could hardly get your breath for admiration. He would answer—they always did—with something like, "But I'm really awfully sweet and shy."

When I asked what I should answer to that, Jonesy said I needn't bother, everything would take care of itself.

The investment was not a sound one for me. I tried it on a boy with whom I had been dancing for a very long time and no help in sight; it was a moment when surefire was needed. There was one disturbing factor I hoped would not deflect my aim. My partner was shorter than I by nearly two inches. Nevertheless, crouching a little, I murmured down at him, with well-rehearsed breathless pauses, "You're—so —big and—*strong*." He, throwing back his head, like a startled fawn, looked up at me wide-eyed.

"You're awfully strong too," he said.

For all our pursuit of trophies, we were as chaste in the hunt as Diana. I venture to assert this in spite of Scott Fitzgerald's chronicles. We were of his era, but not his set. Say I was backward, and I was, but from talking to my contemporaries I know that if a school for backward girls had been established, there were enough of us to fill it. By day we studied English and French literature, philosophy, economics, politics, history of art; intellectually we were reasonably competent. At night, in our bathrobes, while we drank cocoa with marshmallow whip on top, a concoction known locally as "muggle," we discussed religion, careers, marriage and children. Religion was the only factor in our lives that we questioned and into which we probed. We were serenely confident of our success in the others. Sex in itself did not enter into the qualifications we listed for a good marriage. The nearest we came to it was a night I remember at a muggle session when we decided closing your eyes when a boy kissed you was more passionate than looking off into space. "Passionate" was a word frequently used in our conversations.

One spring evening the year of the hygiene lecture, a beau calling on me suggested a walk on the campus. Halfway down an avenue of trees that bordered Senior Row—and I was uneasy about setting foot there because it was a forbidden promenade to all but seniors—my beau suddenly backed me against one of the trees and kissed me "passionately" on the mouth.

On the instant the earth came back under my feet and the sky was overhead again, I was shaken by a convulsion of horror. In that one moment of folly, I had ruined my life and disgraced my family, who had trusted such high hopes to me. I would have to leave college, but I could never go

home. I would run away to live in sordid obscurity. I did run up Senior Row establishing, I am sure, my all-time record of speed. My beau, left behind at the tree trunk, came after me calling, but I outdistanced him. In my room, I applied with great pain the only antidote I could lay hands on. When I was sure there was nothing more I could do, I went downstairs again, uplifted by a sense of noblesse oblige. My betrayer was standing at the foot of the stairs looking up with obviously bewildered anxiety.

"Are you all right?" he called as I reached the landing. I came down the rest of the way and took his hand.

"I hope so," I told him. "I've done everything I could. But no matter what happens," I assured him, "I will never hold you entirely to blame."

Because I could not trust myself to say anything more, I bolted back upstairs but I was sobbing before I reached my door, and I think I did not stop until sometime in the early morning, when I fell asleep.

In the days and nights that followed I prayed fervently, sometimes in snatches, sometimes at length, and one glorious day—I was thoroughly knowledgeable on the distaff side— I knew I was delivered from shame and disgrace. During the interminable time of apprehension and prayer, I had not confided my guilty secret even to my closest friends, but now, jubilant over my successful action, I let it be known that if any girls got into trouble I could help them.

Within a week of my generous and selfless offer exposing my own frailty, I was summoned to the Dean's office. I did not know why I had been sent for but since I had broken no college rules, I went with a light heart. The Dean, with no preliminaries, told me my presence at college was no longer desirable. Chicken Little was afraid the sky would fall on her head; I knew it had fallen. I had breath only for a whispered "Why?" The Dean was astonished, she said, that I should ask, as if my own appalling degradation was not enough to warrant my expulsion. My efforts toward commercializing this unspeakable activity had dragged down the name of the college, subjecting it to a kind of notoriety that could close its doors. What she said was so bewildering, I felt as if I were listening to a language I had never heard before.

"Notoriety?" I echoed, though I still had very little voice. "Why, I've done nothing to bring notoriety—"

She scarcely let me finish the word. "Are you telling me that spreading information about abortion is nothing?"

"Abortion" was a word I was not sure of, but "spreading information" was enlightening. My shameful incident had been discovered and I burst into sobbing incoherence. It had all been so unexpected. Certainly I hadn't meant to do anything that would disgrace the college; I would never let such a thing happen again, but I had thought, perhaps, other girls might have been overtaken as I had been and threatened with a terrible consequence. I wanted to help them by telling them what I had done, because it had worked.

"I want the name of the unspeakable person you have recommended," was her answer. "We shall, of course, report it to the police."

I was on my feet trying to see my way to the door.

"I didn't send them to anyone." I found it hard to shape the words while I was crying. "I just told them what to do."

The Dean suddenly got to her feet, knocking her chair over. I thought she was going to spring at me. Blurred as the image was, I could see she was trembling. Her mouth was open and her eyes looked wild.

Backing away from her, I said, "I would have told them to gargle with peroxide full strength. It burns your mouth terribly but that's what I did."

I had been reaching for the doorknob and could not find it. She put her hand to her forehead and drew it down over her face. When she had taken it away, I saw her whole expression had changed. She looked sad, not wild any more.

"Come back," she said, "and sit down."

I was still uneasy but not so frightened. I went to her desk again, picked up her chair for her. She fairly dropped into it; she seemed weak. She leaned forward, put her elbows on her desk and rested her head between her hands. I had not sat down. I wanted to ensure a quick getaway if she went into a rage again. When she raised her head, to my amazement she was smiling, but sadly; perhaps she felt a little sorry about expelling me and I did not want pity.

"There has been a misunderstanding," she said. "I must give this some further thought. Meantime I will ask you on your honor not to make known our conversation this morning and above all not to make any further offers of assistance to your friends."

I had stopped crying. I could speak but my voice was harsh. "When must I leave college?" I asked.

"You are not going to leave college. As I told you, this was a misunderstanding."

When I had reached the door, she stopped me once more. "Miss Kimbrough," she asked, "have you never talked with your mother about childbirth and procreation?"

"Oh, yes indeed," I told her. "Lots of times."

The widely read syndicated column "Dear Abby," in the *New York Post* of Monday, March 20, 1972, included these communications:

DEAR ABBY: I hope you won't think this is too dumb to answer. Can a girl get pregnant from kissing?

GLORIA

DEAR GLORIA: No. But it's a good beginning.

In the same column:

Confidential to "FROM THE OLD SCHOOL": Welcome to the club. Very few of us who had "old world" parents were told "the facts of life" by our mothers. All my mother told me, God bless her, was never to put bananas in the refrigerator.

Plus ça change, plus c'est la même chose. They just don't listen.